CHRISTIANITY

Judy Perkins and Alan Brown

B T Batsford Ltd   London

© Judy Perkins and Alan Brown 1988
First published 1988

Typeset by Tek-Art Ltd, Kent
and printed and bound by
Richard Clay
Chichester, Sussex
for the publishers
B T Batsford Ltd
4 Fitzhardinge Street
London W1H 0AH

ISBN 0 7134 5319 2

Acknowledgments

The Author and Publishers would like to thank the
following for permission to reproduce copyright
illustrations: C. Adamson, page 42; The British
Library, pages 6, 34, 45; The Camera Press/Karsh
of Ottawa, page 26(a); The Camera Press/Peter
Mitchell, page 31; The Camera Press/Novosti,
page 32; The Camera Press/Alan Whicker, page
19(b); Sue Chapman, pages 8(a), 11, 20, 38(a), 40;
Church Information Service, pages 15, 33(c); Zena
Flax, page 58; Sonia Halliday, frontispiece and
page 16(a); Richard Haynes, page 16(b); Israeli
Government Press Office, page 59; Keystone
Collection, pages 27, 44, 48; The Mandel Archive,
page 41; The Mandel Archive/Charles Quick, page
38(b); The Mansell Collection, pages 18, 26(b),
33(a), 57; Leonard von Matt, page 13; The
National Portrait Gallery, page 37; PACE, page
49(b); Judy Perkins, pages 32, 49(a), 56; Michael
Ryan, pages 25, 39; Salvation Army Information
Services, page 10; Ronald Sheridan, page 47; Tate
Gallery, pages 30(a), 53; USPG, page 22, 29,
33(b); Roger Wood, page 23; World Council of
Churches, pages 9, 24; World Council of
Churches/John Taylor, page 51. The excerpt from
the Nicene Creed on page 21 is © International
Consultation on English Texts (ICET),
reproduced by kind permission of SPCK. The
pictures were researched by Patricia Mandel.

Frontispiece
Good Friday procession in Jerusalem.

Cover Illustrations
The colour photograph shows the Elevation of the
Host in Chichester Cathedral (courtesy John
Rankin); the photograph (*bottom left*) shows a
Baptist minister preaching (courtesy the *Baptist
Times*); the icon of Christ (*bottom right*) is
reproduced by courtesy of the Mansell Collection.

Introduction

Christianity is a worldwide religion which has existed for almost 2000 years, although its roots in the Jewish religion go back even further. During that time it has developed and changed for many reasons – some religious, some political and historical – leading to the separation of various groups from one another. It has been estimated that today there are over 20,000 different groupings within the Christian Church as a whole, encompassing a wide variety of practices and beliefs. It may be helpful to think of "Christianities" rather than "Christianity"; as you read the book you will recognise this diversity.

Despite the variations, however, one element in Christianity is constant: it is a religion of faith and salvation. Christians may express this faith in the form of a creed, a statement of belief, or as a personal relationship with Jesus or in the rites of a particular church or in a combination of all of these. Yet however faith is expressed it focuses on Jesus of Nazareth whom Christians believe to be the saviour of the world. He is more than just a messenger or a prophet; he is the Son of God. The Jews were and are looking forward to a time when God would send a Messiah or saviour, but Christians believe he did so in Jesus. It is not accurate, therefore, to call Jesus the founder of Christianity because he did not found a new religion but develop an old one. All Christians accept the Bible, although they put different interpretations upon it.

About one-third of the world's population is Christian and half of that third Roman Catholic, so it is important to know something of Roman Catholic beliefs and practices. Generally we can think of Christianity as being divided into four great families: Roman Catholic, Orthodox, Protestant and Pentecostal. The one main church that does not fit easily into this grouping is the Anglican Church, which is a bridge, of a sort, between Roman Catholicism and the Protestant churches.

The Christian usage of "B.C." and "A.D." in dates is not accepted by the non-Christian religions. "B.C.E." (Before the Common Era) and "C.E." (Common Era) have become more accepted in recent years.

A Note About the Bible

The Bible is an important book for all Christians, and throughout this dictionary there are many references to it, some of which are quoted in full while others you should check yourself. The reference begins with the name of the book, which can usually be found in an index at the beginning of a Bible. (Watch out for Bibles which go back to page 1 when they get to the New Testament.) All but the shortest books are divided into chapters, and this is the first number given after the name. All books are further divided into verses, usually no more than a few lines long, and the second number refers to the verse. For example, "John 3:16" means the Gospel of *John*, chapter *3*, verse *16*.

Angel

The word "angel" comes from the Greek word for a messenger, and in many Bible stories angels deliver messages from God. For example, Mary was told by the angel Gabriel that she was to have a child (Luke 1:26-38). Angels dwell primarily in heaven and are neither male nor female. They are in no way human, and people do not become angels when they die. Apart from taking messages, the angels' chief task is worshipping God. During the Eucharist (see p. 25) the worship of the people is explicitly joined with that of the angels and of all the company of heaven. Three of the angels are named in the Bible or the Apocrypha (see p. 5); these are Michael, Gabriel and Raphael, who are sometimes called "Archangels".

Some people believe that everyone has a guardian angel who looks after them. This may be thought of as a way of saying that God looks after individuals.

Anglican Church

See *Bible (use)*, *Church buildings*, *Church (history)*, *Church (organization)*, *Eucharist*.

Ascension

According to the Book of Acts, Jesus spent 40 days with the disciples after his resurrection. At the end of this period he told them to stay in Jerusalem and wait for the Holy Spirit; then he was lifted up and a cloud hid him from them (Acts 1:1-11). This is called the Ascension, and it is celebrated 40 days after Easter, so it is always a Thursday. In some churches a Paschal candle (see p. 8) is lit during all the services held from Easter until it is extinguished during the reading of the lessons on Ascension Day. This signifies that the risen Christ is no longer present on earth. The Ascension is important because Jesus took his humanity into God, preparing the way for Christians to follow.

See also *Jesus*.

Authority

One of the questions asked of Jesus, according to the Gospels, was: "By what authority are you acting like this? Who gave you this authority?" (Matthew 21:23). It was an important question because Jesus was teaching what seemed a new interpretation of the Jewish law and the chief priests and elders wanted to know where this teaching came from. They may have wondered if it was from a particular rabbinic school of teaching:

> Jesus replied, "I have a question to ask too; answer it, and I will tell you by what authority I act. The baptism of John: was it from God, or from man?" This set them arguing among themselves: "If we say 'from God', he will say, 'Then why did you not believe him?' But if we say 'from man' we are afraid of the people for they all take John for a prophet." So they answered, "We do not know." And Jesus said, "Then neither will I tell you by what authority I act."
> (Matthew 21:23-27; Mark 11:27-33; and Luke 20:1-8)

In other words, Jesus does not answer the question directly. He wishes his listeners to make up their own minds about where his authority comes from. In the Gospel of John this is made much clearer:

> I rely on a testimony higher than John's [i.e. John the Baptist's]. There is enough to testify that the Father has sent me, in the works my Father gave me to do and to finish – the very works I have in hand. This testimony was given to me by the Father.
> (John 5:36-37)

For Christians, the authority of Jesus comes from God and Jesus in turn gives authority to his followers to act in his name:

> He now called the twelve together and gave them power and authority to overcome all the devils and to cure diseases, and sent them to proclaim the kingdom of God and to heal.
> (Luke 9:1)

The authority Jesus passed on to his 12 apostles is often called the "apostolic succession". This means that these 12 passed on that authority to others, and they on to still more, down through the generations until today.

The Roman Catholic Church believes that the Pope is in direct succession from Peter, to whom Jesus gave special authority (Matthew 16:18-19). Many priests in the Roman Catholic and Anglican Churches would describe themselves as being "under authority", meaning that they accept the authority of their bishop in all things and especially in spiritual and personal matters. Members of the Protestant churches would not regard authority in this way. Generally they believe that *their* authority is taken from the Bible and the word that is preached by the minister or pastor. Consequently there is a great spirit of independence within the Protestant and Reformed traditions (see p. 13) and a belief that the Bible is the ultimate source of authority rather than any priest. This places a much greater emphasis on the individual and his or her personal relationship with God through the Bible and the guidance of the Holy Spirit.

See also *Bible (history)*.

Benediction

"Benediction" has two meanings. In some Protestant churches it is commonly used to mean "blessing", and may refer particularly to the prayer of blessing at the end of a service. In Catholic churches it refers to a service where the people express their devotion to Christ, who is present in the form of a "host" or piece of bread consecrated during a Eucharist (see p. 25). The host is commonly displayed in a stand called a "monstrance", placed on the altar, surrounded by candles and sometimes flowers. Incense is used, hymns are sung and prayers are recited, particularly prayers addressed to Christ. The service ends with the priest blessing the congregation with the host. It is most commonly held in the afternoon and evening.

This service used to be more popular than it is now, because until the Second World War Catholics were required to fast from midnight onwards if they wished to receive Holy Communion. As the priest also had to fast, evening masses were rare. Today the period of fasting has been reduced to an hour, so evening masses are more frequent and have tended to replace Benediction as an evening service.

Bible (history)

The Christian Bible is made up of the Old Testament and the New Testament. The Old Testament is largely the Hebrew Bible (the Bible of the Jews) and numbers 39 books. The New Testament contains 27 documents – four Gospels, the Acts of the Apostles, 21 letters (13 bearing the name of Paul), and the Book of Revelation. The Roman Catholic Church includes the Apocrypha in its Bible in addition to the Old and New Testaments. The Apocrypha (meaning "hidden") is a collection of Jewish literature written during the last two or three centuries B.C.E and provides a useful background to the New Testament. It is not to be found in the Hebrew Bible, however. Generally, Christians, when referring to "the Bible", mean both the Old and New Testaments.

In essence the New Testament represents the writings of Christians in the first generation after the death of Jesus. The Old Testament is interpreted through the New Testament and although the text of it is virtually the same as that of the Hebrew Bible, Christians use it quite differently. The main content of the Hebrew Bible was agreed before the beginning of the Christian era and was finally "sealed" between 70-100 C.E.

A number of other Christian documents were on the verge of being accepted by the early Christian Church. The main outlines of the New Testament canon (the list of books given authority by the Church) were decided on during the second century, although some documents were not universally accepted until quite late. Examples include the Epistle to the Hebrews and the Book of Revelation in particular. The final list was agreed at a Council in Rome, probably in 382 C.E.

The Bible has unique authority among Christians: it occupies a central place in most Christian public worship; it is used as a basic text to preach from; it is appealed to by Christians to establish standards for belief and conduct. Because of its importance the various Christian churches have set out guidelines on how to understand what the Bible says and who has the authority to interpret it correctly. Some Christian churches emphasise that the priests and the Church itself are the only persons able to interpret scripture

The New Testament was originally written in Greek on papyrus. This is a passage from the letter to the Hebrews written by hand in the third or fourth century C.E.

correctly. In the Protestant churches there is generally more emphasis on the right of each individual worshipper to take what meaning is appropriate from the Bible, guided by the Holy Spirit.

Christians continue to discuss how the Bible should be used. Some believe it to be the unchanging word of God: it must be taken literally and cannot be altered. Others believe it is the work of *people*, although inspired by God, and can therefore be questioned and debated.

See also *Authority, Eucharist.*

6

Bible (use)

Public worship

Church services almost always include at least one reading from the Bible. The extract(s) may be chosen by the person leading the service or may follow a reading plan called a "lectionary" – a calendar listing the readings for each day. The readings for occasional services such as weddings and funerals are chosen because they are relevant. For example, at weddings people often choose the Hymn to Love (I Corinthians 13) or the story of the wedding at Cana (John 2:1-11).

Most services include at least two readings. In the Church of England, morning and evening prayer services include readings from both the Old Testament and the New Testament. At the Eucharist (see p. 25) there may be on Old Testament reading as well as, or instead of, a reading from the New Testament letters or Epistles, but there is always a Gospel reading. In Anglican, Catholic and Orthodox churches extra honour paid may be paid to the Gospel; the book may be carried to the middle of the congregation, along with a cross and candles. When the reader, usually a priest or deacon, announces the Gospel he may make the sign of the cross (see p. 22) on the book and the people may follow him in "signing" their foreheads, lips and heart. This shows their intention to keep the words of the Gospel in their minds, on their lips and in their hearts. If incense is used the book will be censed (see p. 32). The congregation remain standing during the reading to signify both their reverence and their readiness to act on what they hear. In the Orthodox Church the bringing in of the Gospel book is called the Little (or Lesser) Entrance.

In churches where the greatest importance is given to preaching, the Bible may be carried into the church at the beginning of the service with some ceremony. The church building itself may also be designed to give prominence to the pulpit from which the Bible is read.

A Bible may be given ceremonially on certain occasions. At ordinations deacons are given a New Testament to show that they have authority to proclaim the Gospel; priests are given a Bible to show their authority to preach the Word of God (see p. 14). At her coronation the Queen was given a Bible, "The most valuable thing that this world affords".

Private worship

It is difficult to say to what extent Christians use the Bible outside Church services. Those who read from it daily may follow the lectionary provided for daily services or they may use notes supplied by one of the Bible-reading societies such as the Scripture Union or the Bible Reading Fellowship which explain or develop the readings. Others may read sections which they choose themselves, sometimes using a commentary to help them understand the text better. Christians who read the Bible at home may read it slowly, then stop to think about what they have read, to see whether it can guide how they live or strengthen what they believe, or encourage them when they are unhappy or uncertain. There are, however, many Christians who go to church but who rarely or never read the Bible at home.

Some Christians meet informally in small groups – often in each other's houses – to study and discuss the Bible together.

Psalms and canticles

The Book of Psalms in the Old Testament is a collection of 150 hymns of various lengths, to be used on various occasions. Traditionally it is said to have been written by King David, although many of the psalms date from a later period. They are stilll used in Christian worship and may be spoken or chanted, or paraphrased and sung as hymns. Psalms form part of every office (see p. 50). Canticles are portions of other books which appear to have been hymns or like hymns originally and which are used in the same way as psalms. They are frequently known by the first word or two from the Latin version, a tradition originating at a time when all services were in Latin. The most widely known include the *Magnificat*, or Song of Mary (Luke 1:46-55), the *Benedictus*, or Song of Zechariah (Luke 1:67-79), and the *Nunc Dimittis*, or Song of Simeon (Luke 2:29-32).

See also *Liturgy, Incense, Prayer Books.*

Candles

Candles of white wax are usually found in Anglican, Catholic and Orthodox churches, particularly on or near the altar. They may also be carried in procession, especially at the entrance and exit of the priest and to the place where the Gospel is read during the Eucharist (see p. 25).

Apart from their functional use in ancient times, candles were also a mark of honour; today, as well as honour they signify welcome to Christ, who is present during the Eucharist. The traditional day on which they are blessed is 2 February, the feast of the Presentation of Christ in the Temple, sometimes called Candlemas. This is because the Nunc Dimittis (see p. 7), especially appropriate on this day, calls Jesus "a light for revelation to the Gentiles".

In some churches there is a stand near a statue or icon (see p. 31) where worshippers may light a small "votive" candle in honour of a saint, perhaps to ask for the saint's continued prayers after the worshipper has left the church. ("Votive" originally referred to something given in fulfilment of a vow but now refers simply to the making of special prayers).

At the Easter vigil a large candle called the Paschal candle is blessed and lighted from the new fire. It has a "chi-rho" (see p. 13), the year and an alpha and omega, as well as five grains of incense at the ends and centre of a cross, to signify the five wounds of Christ on the cross (see picture below). During the service the candle is carried solemnly through the congregation and used to light the candles which everyone is already holding. The candle burns at all services from Easter to Ascension to represent the presence of the risen Christ on earth. After this it is moved near to the font (see p. 15) and lit during baptisms to show that those baptized are to share in the new life of Easter; they may also be given a small candle lit from the Paschal candle.

On the first Sunday in Advent (see p. 10) some churches have Advent carol services; these are often held by candlelight, because at this time Christians prepare for the birth of Jesus, which they think of as a light coming into a dark world. Throughout Advent, churches and families may display a wreath or crown, consisting of four red or purple candles and one white. On the first Sunday

This girl is lighting a "votive" candle in front of a statue of the Virgin Mary. She will leave it in the stand with candles others have left before her.

The large candle on the right of the altar is the Paschal candle. Notice the two smaller candles on the altar.

in Advent one red candle it lit, then on the second two and so on until on Christmas Day the white one is lit as well (see picture on p. 58).

At funerals the coffin may be surrounded by free-standing candles. These are often yellow (unbleached) as a sign of mourning, and are lit to show that although a person's body is dead, his soul is still alive.

Some churches in the Reformed tradition (see p. 12) make no use of candles at all. This is because they stress the importance of the Bible, preaching and individual faith, and do not find this sort of ceremonial and ritual helpful or relevant.

See also *Ascension, Christmas, Easter, Funeral, Initiation.*

This baby is being baptized into the Orthodox Church. The three candles represent the Trinity, and are a sign of new life.

Charismatic

The word "charismatic" comes from the Greek meaning gift. It is often used of a person who is gifted or who has a powerful personality. Christians believe that a charismatic person is someone who has, or claims to have, received the gifts of the Holy Spirit. This refers back to an event in the Acts of the Apostles when the apostles themselves received the gift of the Holy Spirit.

> When the day of Pentecost was running its course they were all together in one place, when suddenly there came from the sky a noise like that of a strong driving wind, which filled the whole house where they were sitting. And there appeared to them tongues like flames of fire, dispersed among them and resting on each one. And they were filled with the Holy Spirit and began to talk in other tongues, as the Spirit gave them utterance.
> (Acts 2:1-4)

"Speaking in tongues" can happen to individuals who feel moved by the Spirit. This is called "glossolalia" and means that the person can speak in many languages – some perhaps unknown to the hearers or even the speaker.

Charismatic churches can be found in most of the Christian denominations but the Pentecostal churches tend to be particularly associated with speaking in tongues. These are still the most rapidly growing of Christian churches though many other denominations have strong charismatic elements.

The general features of charismatic worship in addition to the above are free prayer – perhaps led by a preacher but with the congregation joining in – as well as acts of healing and a frequent use of and reference to the Bible. Some groups identify illness with demonic possession and the casting out of the Devil in the name of Christ can take place.

See also *Pentecost.*

Charity

To Christians the word "charity" means "to give freely with love", and "almsgiving" has come to mean "charitable giving", usually in support of the poor. Charity is not compulsory, otherwise it could not be given freely, but many Christians work for or support charitable organizations or perform local and often private acts of charity. Perhaps the best known form of almsgiving in the West was the establishment of almshouses for the poor, begun many centuries ago. These can still be seen in many towns and villages.

The commitment of Christians to charity is most clearly summed up by St Paul in his first letter to the Corinthians. Compare the Authorized Version of the Bible: "And now abideth faith, hope, charity, these three; but the greatest of these is charity" (1 Corinthians 13:13), with the New English Bible: "In a word, there are three things that last for ever: faith hope and love; but the greatest of them all is love" (1 Corinthians 13:13). Charity and love can be interchangeable for many Christians. It is not simply the giving which characterizes charity but the Christian love that lies behind and motivates the act of giving.

The Salvation Army is well known for its charitable caring activities. It runs hostels for the homeless and traces people separated from their families as part of its charitable mission.

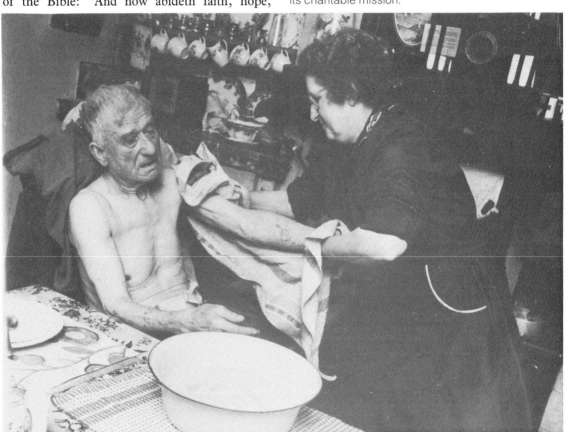

Christmas

Advent
The Christian year begins with the first Sunday in Advent – the fourth Sunday before Christmas. "Advent" means "coming" and it is a time to prepare for the coming of Christmas and look forward to Christ's Second Coming. The period of Advent has been part of the Christmas cycle of festival since the sixth century C.E.

Advent is a solemn but hopeful time. In church,

readings from the Old Testament look forward to the coming of a saviour. In many Christian homes and churches an Advent Crown is displayed, containing four candles, and sometimes five (one for Christmas). On each of the four Sundays of Advent another candle is lit to symbolize the approaching light of the birth of the Saviour. Although Christmas has not yet arrived many churches and schools hold carol services during this season.

Christmas

Although Easter is the major festival of the Christian year, Christmas is the most widely celebrated. The word "Christmas" derives from the Old English *Christes maesse* or "Christ's Mass". For Christians, Christmas is the time to celebrate the coming of God's son to earth, born of Mary his mother. This is regarded as the greatest gift God could give to all his people, so Christmas is a time of great thanksgiving.

On Christmas Eve many Christians attend a Midnight Mass in their church, which is usually specially decorated. A crib scene is often set up, illustrating the traditional scene of the birth of Jesus as recorded in the Gospels of Matthew

(Chapter 1) and Luke (Chapter 2). This custom, which is thought to have been first introduced by St Francis of Assisi in 1223 C.E., has now become universal. The figure of the infant Jesus is in a manger or crib, surrounded by Mary, Joseph, the shepherds and wise men plus various animals, such as oxen, asses and sheep.

The two biblical accounts of the birth of Jesus differ markedly: in Luke's account his birth is told to the shepherds in the field, who hear that Jesus was born in a stable because there was no room in the inn. Matthew's account refers to wise men or "magi" coming from the East, following a star and bringing gifts of gold, frankincense and myrrh: gold for a king, incense for God and myrrh to symbolize suffering. (At the time, myrrh was an ointment used in laying out the dead.) The two accounts agree about the names of Jesus, Mary and

The crib scene has become traditional in most churches. It is believed that it was started by St Francis in the thirteenth century C.E. and it provides a focus for remembering the events of the birth of Jesus.

Joseph and that Bethlehem was the place of birth.

The early Christian Church did not celebrate Christmas. Indeed, its date was fixed only early in the fourth century C.E. It seems to have replaced the Roman festival celebrating the birth of Mithras (sometimes called the birth of the Unconquerable Sun) during the reign of the first Christian Roman emperor, Constantine. No one knows the exact day when Jesus was born. Many of the traditions associated with Christmas in the West – Christmas trees, yule logs and mistletoe – developed either from pre-Christian religions or from cultural customs. Carols, for example, were originally songs for dancing.

The eastern Orthodox churches originally celebrated the birth and baptism of Jesus on 7 January. However, the influence of Rome persuaded most churches to accept 25 December as the date, although some still celebrate Christmas on 7 January (the Armenian Orthodox Church, for example).

Epiphany

Either the Sunday after Epiphany or Candlemas (see p. 8) marks the end of the Christmas festival. "Epiphany" means "manifestation" (or "showing forth") and in the early Christian Church it referred to God's power revealed in Jesus as Son of God at his baptism. By the fourth century C.E. the eastern Orthodox churches celebrated three manifestations at Epiphany: the birth of Jesus, his baptism and his first miracle (the changing of water to wine at Cana of Galilee [John 2:1-11]).

In the West, Epiphany came to commemorate the adoration of the magi and the manifestation of Christ to the Gentiles. In the East, Epiphany still commemorates the baptism of Jesus. In the Ethiopian Church, on the eve of Epiphany the Holy Arks of the Covenant are processed through the streets. These Arks are stone tablets with the Gospels inscribed on them. The congregation then gathers together to spend the night in prayer before the celebrations of Epiphany.

Church (history)

The word used for the Christian community in the early Church was "*ecclesia*", from which the word "ecclesiastical" comes, meaning "things to do with the church". Christians use the word to mean different things but here we are particularly concerned with the idea of the church as a worldwide community of Christians.

In the early Christian Church there were small groups of believers in many towns and cities, but no overall organization of these groups. As time passed, these communities grew in number and spread over a wider area, and a more definite organizational shape began to emerge. During the first two or three centuries cities like Rome, Antioch, Alexandria and, later, Constantinople became great Christian centres under the control and care of a bishop. The western church under the authority of the Bishop of Rome came to have a different character from the eastern "Orthodox" churches, based largely on cultural and political differences between them. A split arising in the seventh century and completed in 1054 C.E., created the first real division between the branches of the Christian Church.

At the time of the Reformation in Europe, during the sixteenth century C.E., a number of movements sprang up in opposition to the Roman Catholic Church. This led to the establishment of Calvinist and Lutheran churches (following the teachings of Jean Calvin, a Frenchman, and Martin Luther, a German). The Church of England removed itself from the rule of the Roman Catholic Church during the sixteenth century, and other groups like the Methodists and the Society of Friends developed in later centuries. The Roman Catholic Church, the Orthodox Church and some Protestant churches each claim to be the sole and only true church on earth. This leads to debate and argument over which, if any, represents the true teaching of Christ. Virtually all Christians, however, accept that the title "Body of Christ" refers to *all* Christians who respond in some way to the life of Jesus Christ. It is a term which binds together Christians in a mystical way, helping them to cope with divisions and differences between them.

The Orthodox Church is made up of many national and regional churches, linked with the Greek-speaking churches of the eastern Roman Empire. Today there are Russian, Serbian, Armenian and Greek Orthodox churches, for example, each with their own hierarchy of patriarchs, bishops and councils (see p. 14). It includes four ancient patriarchates: Alexandria, Antioch, Constantinople and Jerusalem. Its religious life centres on the sacraments (see p. 54).

The Roman Catholic Church was the main church in the West until the sixteenth century, when Protestantism became a major feature of Christian life, especially in northern Europe.

Lutheran churches were founded in German-speaking countries and Scandinavia; Calvinist (or Reformed) churches were strong in France, Switzerland, Scotland, the Netherlands. The Church of England has many practices which are similar to those of the Roman Catholic Church but it also has some affinities with the smaller Protestant churches, such as the Free Churches of Baptists, Presbyterians and Congregationalists (some Presbyterians and Congregationalists have now joined to form the United Reformed Church). Methodism arose from the preaching of John Wesley, an Anglican priest, becoming particularly strong in industrial areas of the north of England and southern Wales. During its early decades it

The Chi-Rho symbol was the banner of Constantine, the first Christian Roman Emperor. Chi and Rho (X and P) are the first two letters of the Greek word for Christ. On the left of the Chi is an Alpha and on the right an Omega. These are the first and last letters of the Greek alphabet, and stand for Christ the beginning and the end (Revelation 21:6).

fragmented into other smaller churches, and gave rise to the Salvation Army. Today, the Methodist Church is united again, although the Salvation Army has continued along its own path. Other Protestant denominations include the Society of Friends (the Quakers) and the various Pentecostal churches, which form the fastest growing group of churches today, particularly in Africa.

Church (organization)

John records the example set by Jesus at the Last Supper when he washed the disciples feet, despite Peter's protests (John 13:3-17). Jesus said to them:

> Then if I, your Lord and Master, have washed your feet, you also ought to wash one another's feet. I have set you an example: you are to do as I have done for you. In very truth I tell you, a servant is not greater than his master, nor a messenger than the one who sent him. If you know this, happy are you if you act upon it. (John 13:14-17)

Thus ministry and service have been important ideals for all Christians, but especially for those who lead the Church. In some churches these leaders are believed to be the spiritual heirs of the men to whom Jesus spoke the words above. This is known as a belief in the "apostolic succession" (see p. 4). Roman Catholics, Anglicans and Orthodox Christians all believe that their ancient orders of bishop, priest and deacon form a chain which goes back to the apostles.

Deacons are ordained by their bishop; as their historic role includes the reading of the Gospel they are usually given a New Testament to symbolise this. Deacons are members of the "diaconate" who used to have the important job of collecting and distributing alms. In the West the diaconate is now usually just a step on the way to becoming a priest, but the Orthodox Church has continued to have permanent deacons. Women are ordained as deacons in the Church of England, but cannot become priests.

Priests are ordained by their bishop and other priests and their functions include celebrating the Eucharist, blessing, giving absolution and administering most of the other sacraments. Some priests who work in schools, colleges, hospitals, the armed forces and in similar institutions are called chaplains, a word applied to people of other faiths doing a similar job. Chaplains in the Army, Navy and Air Force are sometimes called "Padre".

Bishops are consecrated by other bishops, and placed in charge of a *diocese*, the Church name for an administrative area. The city in which a cathedral is situated is called the bishop's "see" (meaning "seat" or "throne"). Bishops have the tasks of priests, but they also confirm and ordain people. Some dioceses have more than one bishop; one is called the diocesan bishop and the others assistants or "suffragans". In the Greek Church bishops are called Metropolitans.

Dioceses are divided into *parishes* in the charge of a priest called a vicar, a rector or a parish priest. He may be helped by another priest or deacon called a curate. Dioceses are grouped in geographical areas called *provinces*, and the bishop of the principal diocese may be called an Archbishop.

The head of the whole Roman Catholic Church is the Pope, who is also the Bishop of Rome. The first Bishop of Rome was St Peter and the Pope's supremacy is based on the words of Jesus to St Peter: "You are Peter, and on this rock I will build my church" (Matthew 16:18). Recalling the words of Jesus quoted earlier, another title for the Pope is the "servant of the servants of Christ". The Orthodox churches do not have a worldwide organization, but each church is headed by a bishop called a Patriarch. All the patriarchs have equal authority. The head of the Church of England is the Queen, although certain powers are also held by Parliament. The Queen appoints bishops and archbishops with advice from the Prime Minister, but in many other countries, such as Wales and Canada, Anglican bishops are elected by the clergy. The various branches of the Anglican Church together form a loose association known as the Anglican Communion. Each of the home countries of the United Kingdom has its own Anglican church.

Cathedrals are run by a dean with a group of priests called canons, known collectively as the "chapter". In the Church of England the dean and chapter are independent of the bishop, who is in charge of the diocese but not of the cathedral. This may be shown on ceremonial occasions by the bishop knocking on the door of the cathedral and asking to be admitted.

In the churches discussed so far, the term "minister" may be used but its meaning varies and it usually applies to people only while they are performing a certain function. In other churches, like the Methodist Church, the term, however, is commonly used for any clergyman. This is often in preference to the term "priest", because some Christians dislike the idea that they need anyone to mediate between them and God. They may express this equality before God as the "priesthood of all believers".

Some churches may have "elders" with either spiritual or administrative roles; this is very important in the Baptist Church which gives great independence to the local church. Elders are not necessarily old, but their title reflects their wisdom.

The Methodist Church, in contrast to this, has a centralized structure in which churches are grouped into *circuits*; these in turn are grouped into *districts*. The supreme Methodist authority is the Conference, of which there is one in most countries. The Lutheran churches in Europe are organized by country, often with the head of state as the head of the church. Ministers and areas roughly equivalent to dioceses are supervised by bishops or "superintendants", although in this case "bishop" implies an administrative rather than spiritual authority. "Pastor" is a word which means "shepherd" and it is used in some churches in place of "minister". It reflects the care that the minister has for his people, as in the relationship of a shepherd and his flock.

Some churches are completely independent of all organized authority. These usually meet in simple buildings and have names such as the "Evangelical Free Church". Such churches are always evangelical (see p. 42), they often have no full-time minister but are run by members of the congregation.

See also *Church (buildings), Sacrament.*

Church buildings

Church buildings vary enormously in architectural style, reflecting different styles of worship. Most churches are designed to allow a group of people to meet, listen, pray, sing and celebrate baptisms (see p. 32) and the Eucharist (see p. 25). This usually requires the presence of seating, a reading desk, a musical instrument, a table or altar and a font or pool. Some churches may have a pulpit from which sermons are preached as well as a place from which the Bible is read. Many churches face east, because the rising sun is a symbol of the resurrection of Jesus. The ground-plan may be cross-shaped or rectangular; it may be a large rectangle with a smaller rectangle at one end, or a more complex shape.

The arrangement of the furniture inside depends on both the denomination of the church and the design of the building. It is customary for Anglican and Catholic churches to have rows of seats or pews facing the altar. This used to be placed against the east wall, but recent changes in worship have meant that in many cases it has been pulled away from it. If it is firmly fixed, a second altar may have been installed. New churches are often built with the altar nearer the centre and pews or chairs on three or even four sides. This is so that when a priest is celebrating the Eucharist he can stand behind the altar and face the people, increasing the feeling that the congregation is gathered around a table. The reading desk and pulpit are placed on either side of the altar. The traditional place for the font is near the door, to symbolize that entry to the community of the Church is through baptism.

Some churches have one or more chapels, like little churches, with their own altars. These may be used for services where only a small number of people are present or by people who go into the church on their own and want a quiet place to think or pray. Churches in colleges, hospitals, schools,

This is a modern Anglican church. There are chairs rather than pews but the font is near the entrance and the altar is the focal point. The pulpit is on the left and a simple reading desk on the right. A chair is in the middle for the priest to use during the first part of the Eucharist.

castles, large houses and so on are also called chapels.

In many churches there may be a place where confessions are heard, whether a room, a confessional box or a quiet corner. An organ or piano may be situated near the altar or, less commonly, in a gallery at the back of the church. The church choir often has special seating, frequently near the altar.

Some of the bread consecrated in the Eucharist may be kept in the church, and taken to people who are housebound, allowing them to take communion. This store is known as the "reserved sacrament" and it is kept either in a wall safe (an "aumbry") or on the altar, in a locked cupboard known as a "tabernacle".

The windows of a church are often of stained glass, showing incidents in the life of Jesus or representations of the saints. Apart from its beauty, stained glass was important for teaching in the days when most people could not read. (Most modern stained glass, however, is abstract.) Other decoration inside a church may include pictures or statues of Jesus and the saints, most commonly of the Virgin Mary and the patron saint of the church. Not all Christians think that this is a good thing: some believe that it breaks the commandment forbidding the making of idols. Some churches may have a series of Stations of the Cross – 12 or 14 pictures or numbers representing the last few hours before Jesus died.

A room called the "vestry" or "sacristy" is where the priest and other people may change clothes, and where other items may be stored. At the west end of a church there is often a tower or steeple which can be seen for some distance. This symbolizes Man's reaching up to God. It sometimes houses a bell (or bells) which calls people to church. This was important in the days when clocks and watches were rare. Bells may also ring in celebration, as after a wedding.

Orthodox churches have very few seats in them, because Orthodox Christians stand throughout their services and often move around to light candles or greet friends. A large screen called an "iconostasis" divides the people from the altar. It symbolizes the separation of Man from God as a result of Man's sin (see p. 56). There are doors which are opened, however, to show that through Jesus God has opened the way of salvation. There are many icons in an Orthodox church, and it is believed that those painted are actually present (see p. 31). The choir is important in the Orthodox service because there is no instrumental accompaniment and the congregation does not usually sing much. An Orthodox church may have a bell tower and the roof may be domed.

The design of many nonconformist churches shows the importance of preaching: a raised pulpit is placed in the centre of the church at the front. Below this is the Communion table, which is central but less prominent. The organ and the choir may also be situated at the front, so that the overall effect is a bit like that in a theatre. A common feature of these churches is a gallery running around three sides. There are unlikely to be any pictures or statues within the church, but scriptural texts may be displayed in prominent

The Church of Santa Sophia in Constantinople, which was built in the sixth century C.E. The minarets were added in the fifteenth century when it became a mosque.

A Quaker meeting house. The chairs are arranged in a circle because there is no one person who is in charge or leading the worship. The children may leave after a short time to go to Sunday School.

places, along with a plain cross. There may be a font or a pool for baptisms; pools are set into the floor and must be drained and covered when not in use. Nonconformist (or Free) churches used to be called "chapels" – and still are in some parts of Britain, particularly in Wales.

The Salvation Army meets in buildings called "citadels" which are similar to nonconformist churches, but which do not have a Communion table or font. Their flag is displayed in a prominent place and there has to be plenty of room for the Army band. One feature of the citadel is the "mercy seat", which is used especially for praying and for talking to people who have just decided that they want to be Christians.

Quakers congregate in buildings called "meeting houses" which are usually very simple, with chairs arranged in a hollow square. A table with some flowers or a Bible on it may be placed within the meeting house. Some Christians meet at home rather than in special buildings. Usually evangelical, such Christians regard the Bible as their only source of authority (see p. 5).

A cathedral is a church containing the bishop's throne or "*cathedra*". Every diocese has a cathedral and most are very grand and impressive. The medieval cathedrals in this country, which were Roman Catholic originally, were taken over by the Church of England after the Reformation (see p. 13). The Roman Catholic Church in Britain then had no cathedral of its own until the middle of the nineteenth century. New cathedrals are still built. An interesting case is that of Liverpool, where during this century both the Church of England and the Roman Catholic Church have built cathedrals in the same street. Coventry Cathedral was virtually destroyed during the Second World War and a new cathedral has been built next to the ruins of the old building. It includes fine examples of modern art in its stained glass windows, tapestries, stonework and sculpture. This contrasts with many of the older cathedrals which were built and extended over long periods of time, thus including features from various periods.

Shifts in the population lead to some problems with church buildings. There are far too many churches in many city centres where people work but no longer live, as in the old City of London, where services are held only on weekdays. It is usually impossible to sell or demolish these churches and build something else in their place because they are often very old and therefore important from an historical or architectural point of view.

Occasionally, new uses are found for disused or "redundant" churches. These may become centres for study or for exhibitions. The famous London church of St John's, in Smith Square, is used for holding classical music concerts which are often broadcast. One church in Norwich has a collection of brasses which helps to introduce people to brass-rubbing. Some buildings may be taken over by other Christian denominations, or by people of other faiths. For example, some churches have become mosques. In London, at 59 Brick Lane, there is a building which was first a church, then became a synagogue and is now a mosque. The church of Santa Sophia in Constantinople was built in the sixth century and converted into a mosque in the fifteenth century; today it is a museum.

Shifts in population cause problems in the country too. It is common to see an isolated church with few neighbouring buildings. One solution is to make a single clergyman responsible for several churches, with the result that some cannot hold a service every week.

While some churches are no longer needed, new ones are built in new housing estates on the edges of towns and in new towns. This can provide a chance for different denominations to share a building in a way unknown earlier this century. These "community churches" reflect not only the practical advantage of building and maintaining a single structure but also the growing desire of many Christians to work together more closely.

See *Ecumenism*.

Commandments

The Ten Commandments are found first in the Book of Exodus (20:1-17). They form the basis of both Jewish and Christian codes of conduct, though both religions have developed them over the centuries. Briefly the Commandments cover ten areas of belief and practice:

Accept there is one God.
Do not worship idols.
Do not use God's name irreverently.
Keep the sabbath day as a holy day.

Honour your father and mother.
Do not commit murder.
Do not commit adultery.
Do not steal.
Do not tell lies.
Do not want other people's possessions.

The first four Commandments relate specifically to each person's relationship with God; the other six put that relationship within the context of a living community. These rules are repeated again, with small changes, in Exodus 34 and Deuteronomy 5:6-21. They are summed up in Deuteronomy 6:4: "Hear O Israel the Lord is our God, one Lord and you must love the Lord your God with all your heart and soul and strength."

In the New Testament Jesus encourages a lawyer to answer his own question:

"Master, what must I do to inherit eternal life?" Jesus replied, "What is written in the Law? What is your reading of it?" He replied, "Love the Lord your God with all your heart, with all your soul, with all your strength, and with all your mind; and your neighbour as yourself."

"That is the right answer" said Jesus; "do that and you will live."
(Luke 10:26-28; see also Matthew 22:36-40)

In another passage Jesus adds to this. A man comes to him and asks what he must do to inherit eternal life. Jesus tells him to keep to the Commandments. The man replies that he *has* kept to them:

"Where do I fall short?". Jesus said to him, "If you wish to go the whole way, go, sell your possessions, and give to the poor, and then you will have riches in heaven; and come, follow me." When the young man heard this, he went away with a heavy heart; for he was a man of great wealth."
(Matthew 19:21-22)

One of the great Christian teachers, St Augustine, said "Love God and do as you like", meaning that if you love God you would never want to do anything that would hurt anyone else.

This very old-fashioned picture of Moses carrying the tablets of stone down from Mount Sinai is typical of the nineteenth century. The Ten Commandments are engraved on stone, and Moses still glows from being so close to God.

Community

For about 300 years after the life of Jesus there were no church buildings. Christian communities were dotted about the Mediterranean world (and beyond it) meeting in each other's houses or in the open air. The New Testament contains a number of letters written by Paul and others to some of these groups. The Epistles teach, warn, ask for prayers and try to maintain the new faith of the Christian communities.

Although these communities were widespread they felt it necessary to keep in touch with each other to sustain their faith and share their common belief in Jesus. In spite of the various differences between denominations today this is still largely true, particularly at special times of the year such as Christmas, when carol services are often shared, and Easter. In recent years the different churches have begun to meet on a local scale for Bible study. A Week of Prayer for Christian Unity is held annually from 18-25 January.

Within the early Christian communities some people felt that they should devote themselves solely to the service of God. Several "renounced the world" to live as hermits, without possessions, devoting themselves to prayer. St Antony in Egypt is supposed to have been the first to do so. (Interestingly, the word "monk" comes from the Greek word meaning "alone".) In centuries to come increasing numbers of men and women (who were called nuns) renounced the world and began to form separate communities. Some of these communities grew to a large size and had thousands of members.

Probably the best known order of monks in the West are the Benedictines, named after St Benedict. He drew up a set of rules for the monastic life – called the Rule of St Benedict – which has remained valid for virtually all Christian monastic orders. He insisted upon vows of poverty, chastity (no sexual relations) and obedience; monks were expected to pray many times during the day and to work hard. Originally, prayers were said daily from 2.00am to 8.00pm but four separate prayer times (or "offices") are more usual today.

The Jesuits, a well known teaching order founded by St Ignatius Loyola in the sixteenth century, add to those three vows a special vow of obedience to the Pope, the Supreme Bishop of the Roman Catholic Church. The proper name for the Jesuits is the Society of Jesus; they have a long history of carrying out educational work within the Roman Catholic Church.

The Franciscans, a thirteenth-century foundation, took their name from St Francis of Assisi. They were soon followed by the Poor Clares. St Clare was a contemporary of St Francis in Assisi and, like him, she led a life of prayer and poverty. There are still many different monastic orders within the Christian churches; the Dominicans (named after St Dominic) are another large order.

Other forms of religious community exist. The Taizé Community in France has members from many different Christian denominations, though all its members are monks. To be a member of the Iona Community does not mean that you have to become a monk or a nun. With its headquarters on the Scottish island of Iona its members have "normal" occupations and come from all over Britain and beyond. The men and women who belong to this community commit themselves to pray regularly at set times – for each other and for the world. Members are also committed to work for peace and to give a part of their income to the community. Some communities have "tertiaries", set up along these lines, consisting of lay people who commit themselves to follow a rule or discipline in their lives.

All nuns engage in some kind of work, and for contemplatives it is often simple manual work to enable them to be self-sufficient as far as possible.

The traditional black habit is less familiar today. Here a novice sits apart from the fully professed nuns during worship. She has not yet made her lifelong vows.

Confession

Confession or "reconciliation" refers to the ministry in which a Christian makes a confession before a priest who in turn gives "absolution" or forgiveness. It is one of the seven sacraments (see p. 54) of the Catholic Church, and is used frequently in the Orthodox Church and sometimes in the Church of England.

According to John's Gospel, Jesus appeared to the disciples on the evening of Easter Day and said, "Receive the Holy Spirit. If you forgive the sins of any they are forgiven; if you retain the sins of any they are retained" (John 20:23). In churches which believe in the "apostolic succession" (see p. 4) this authority is believed to be vested in priests.

Before going to confession a Christian will try to remember all the sins he or she has committed since the last confession. He or she may read part of the teaching of Jesus, such as the Sermon on the Mount, or use a list of questions for self-examination and try to think of ways in which he or she has failed. A Christian must make a complete confession and not miss anything out deliberately, although if something is genuinely forgotton it will not matter. It is important that steps should be taken to make amends for particular failures: a Christian should apologize for being rude or bad-tempered, and replace anything which is taken. He or she must be sorry, and intend not to do the same again.

Confessions are usually heard in church, and may be formal or informal. The person confessing is called a "penitent", a word connected with "repentance". In a formal confession the penitent will kneel next to the priest, who is seated. This may take place in a box, designed so that they can hear but not see each other, or in a quiet corner of the church. The priest blesses the penitent, who then reads his or her confession. The penitent says that he or she is sorry and begs forgiveness. The priest may ask questions if something is unclear and will also give some advice. The priest then gives the penitent a penance, usually a prayer or psalm to say or a part of the Bible to read. This is not a punishment, but a sign of repentance. The priest then pronounces the absolution and gives his blessing. As he dismisses the penitent he says, "Pray for me, a sinner also." This is to show that he is not sitting in judgement on the penitent; he will also make his confession to a priest.

In an informal confession, priest and penitent sit together in a private room; more conversation takes place, although there may still be a formal confession at the beginning or at the end. No priest

The priest raises his hand to give absolution at the end of the confession. In this church there is a curtain which the penitent may close or leave open. This penitent prefers to see the priest face-to-face but if she preferred to remain anonymous she would close the curtain.

will ever repeat anything told to him in this way; this is called the "seal of the confessional" and priests have gone to prison rather than break it.

Occasionally, confession may be heard out of doors. This occurs mainly during pilgrimages (see p. 48) in warm countries, either because the available church is not big enough or because there is no church in the area.

Many Christians value this sacrament because they are assured that their sins are forgiven and can be put behind them; they also value the chance it gives them to reassess their life and receive advice. It is rather like a spiritual spring-cleaning.

See also *Sacrament*.

Consecration

Consecration means "being made holy", and can be applied to people or things set aside for God. It is most commonly used of the bread and wine of the Eucharist becoming the body and blood of Christ, of the making of bishops and of the blessing of church buildings and their contents.

See also *Eucharist*.

Creeds

Christianity is a religion that is concerned with belief. In the first few centuries after the life of Jesus the Christian Church tried to set down its basic beliefs. There were two main reasons for this. First, when new Christians were baptized they were expected to (and were willing to) confess their faith in Jesus. Out of these baptismal formulae developed more formal statements of faith called "creeds". Secondly, there was a need to sort out what the Christian believed from what others believed about Jesus and his relationship to God. A creed helped to defend the Church against false beliefs.

There are two main creeds which date from the early centuries of the Church: the Apostles' Creed and the Nicene Creed. Both are still used in worship in many churches. The Apostles' Creed is so-called because tradition says that each part was made up by a different apostle (this is no longer generally believed), and it is used in both Roman Catholic and Anglican churches. The Nicene Creed is based on a formula agreed at the Council of Nicaea in 325 C.E. It is more elaborate than the Apostles' Creed and is often used at the Eucharist (see p. 25) in Roman Catholic and Anglican churches and at baptisms in the Orthodox Church. Another, less frequently used, creed is the Athanasian Creed, named after Bishop Athenasius (*c*.296-373 C.E.) although it was written later; its exact origins are unknown.

In the Protestant churches creeds are less used. The term "Confession of Faith" is more common; the Lutheran Augsburg Confession and the Presbyterian Westminster Confession are two of the best known examples (both are statements of what the particular church believes). The Baptists, generally, have been reluctant to use creeds in worship.

The Nicene Creed

We believe in one God,
the Father, the almighty,
maker of heaven and earth,
of all that is,
seen and unseen.

We believe in one Lord, Jesus Christ,
the only Son of God,
eternally begotten of the Father,
God from God, Light from Light,
true God from true God,
begotten, not made,
of one Being with the Father.
Through him all things were made.
For us men and for our salvation
he came down from heaven;
by the power of the Holy Spirit
he became incarnate of the Virgin Mary,
    and was made man.
For our sake he was crucified under
    Pontius Pilate;
he suffered death and was buried.

On the third day he rose again
in accordance with the Scriptures;
he ascended into heaven
and is seated at the right hand of the Father.
He will come again in glory
to judge the living and the dead,
and his kingdom will have no end.

We believe in the Holy Spirit,
the Lord, the giver of life,
who proceeds from the Father and the Son.
With the Father and the Son he is worshipped
    and glorified.
He has spoken through the Prophets.

We believe in one holy catholic
    and apostolic Church.
We acknowledge one baptism for the
    forgiveness of sins.
We look for the resurrection of the dead,
and the life of the world to come. Amen.

Cross

The cross is the most common symbol of Christianity, representing the cross on which Jesus died. Some Christians prefer a plain cross without a figure of Jesus, because they say that Jesus is risen and the cross should therefore be empty. If it has a figure of the dying Jesus on it, the cross is called a "crucifix". Crucifixes are found in many western churches, although some Christians object to them because they believe they violate the commandment which forbids the making of images and idols. In the Orthodox churches crosses are flat but have a picture of Jesus painted on them. Less common is a cross with a figure of Jesus crowned and wearing priestly vestments; this is known by the Latin name *Christus Rex*, Christ the King, representing Jesus glorified.

Where crucifixes are found there are often several in a church. There is usually one on or near each altar, one over the pulpit, one where confessions are heard and one in the vestry. There may also be a processional cross, on a long pole, which can be carried at the head of processions. Christians may have a crucifix at home as well, perhaps in the bedroom where they can see it as they pray.

Crosses made from precious metal or even wood are sometimes worn on a chain. They are often given as presents to mark an event such as confirmation. Bishops often wear a large silver cross, as do monks and nuns, even in orders which no longer wear a distinctive habit (the traditional clothing for monks and nuns).

Some Christians make the sign of the cross on their body. In the West this is done with the right hand, touching the forehead, stomach, left side of chest then the right side. In the East the right side is touched before the left. There are many occasions when this is done: at the beginning and end of prayers, when being blessed or absolved, before receiving Holy Communion and when blessing oneself with holy water. It is connected with the formula, "In the name of the Father [forehead] and of the Son [stomach] and of the Holy Ghost [chest], Amen."

The usual form of a cross is a T with an upright extending beyond the arms. Other forms include an X (the cross of St Andrew, who according to tradition was crucified in that form) and a cross on top of three steps which are said to represent faith, hope and love.

The two figures at the foot of the cross are Mary, mother of Jesus, and John the "beloved disciple". According to John's gospel, Jesus gave Mary into John's care (John 20:26-27). The letters "INRI" are an abbreviation of the Latin words "*Iesus Nazarenus Rex Iudaeorum*", "Jesus of Nazareth, King of the Jews", which the Romans nailed to the cross (John 20:19).

Death

Traditionally, Christians believe that their soul continues to live on after death: those who are judged to be worthy go to heaven; those who are judged to be unworthy go to hell for punishment. Roman Catholics believe that a few souls go straight to be with God (this is called the "beatific vision") and that the remainder of saved souls have to undergo a period of purification in "purgatory"; this view is not shared by the Protestant churches.

At the end of time, it is believed, Jesus will come again (the Second Coming) and there will be a new Jerusalem where all Christians will live. The dead will be resurrected and at the Second Coming there will be the Last Judgement. This will decide whether the soul finally goes to heaven or hell for all eternity. Hell is often depicted artistically as a fiery furnace where souls are tormented by devils. This may be illustrated by the parable of Dives and Lazarus in Luke 16:19 where Dives, the rich man, is tormented in hell whereas Lazarus, the poor man, is in heaven. Dives pleads with Abraham, with whom Lazarus is, to send Lazarus "to dip the tip of his finger in water, to cool my tongue for I am in agony in this fire" (verse 24).

In present times heaven and hell tend to be described in other ways, heaven as a place of absolute bliss, where one is in communion with God, and hell as the opposite – the despair and misery of separation from God. Some Christians believe that there will not be eternal punishment, because God is love, and that in the end everyone, even the most evil, will be saved.

See also *Funeral*.

This icon of "The Ladder of Climax" is from St Catherine's Monastery on Mount Sinai in Egypt. It shows the righteous ascending to heaven while demons claim the wicked and pull them down to hell.

Easter

Easter is the most important festival of the Christian year. It is when Christians celebrate the resurrection of Jesus, and as St Paul said, "If Christ has not been raised, your faith is futile and you are still in your sins." (I Corinthians 15:17). In other words, Easter is when Christians celebrate the most essential part of their faith. It may seem to the non-Christian that Christmas is more important because it is more widely celebrated, with presents, cards and parties. While the birth of Jesus is important it is his resurrection which Christians believe showed that he is the Son of God.

The name "Easter" is probably connected with the Anglo-Saxon goddess of spring, Eostre. The date varies considerably from year to year and is not the same throughout the world. In the West Easter falls on the first Sunday after the full moon which occurs on or after 21 March; thus it may be as late as 24 April. The date is determined by the moon because Jesus died at the time of the Jewish festival of Passover, and the Jewish calendar is lunar.

The first celebration of Easter usually occurs during the previous evening or early in the morning, before dawn. This is because the women who found the tomb of Jesus empty went there before sunrise; thus the Resurrection must have taken place during the night (Matthew 28). In the Anglican, Catholic and Orthodox traditions elaborate ceremonies centre on darkness, light, water and the Eucharist (see p. 25). This service is called a "vigil" and begins with the church in darkness so that it may not be possible to see even how many people are present. One or two candles illuminate a bible from which a series of extracts are read, concentrating on stories of God giving new life. Everybody has a candle, but it is not yet lit. After the readings the priest lights a fire at the back of the church or in the churchyard, and from this he lights the Paschal candle (see p. 8). The candle is taken to the front of the church in a solemn procession which stops three times for the priest to sing "The light of Christ", to which the people reply, "Thanks be to God". A few people have their candles lit each time, and pass the light from one to another. From the front of the church you can see the light gradually spreading, like a firework in slow motion. A hymn is sung by the priest in praise of God, and the water in the font is blessed.

At one time Easter was the only period of the year during which baptisms were allowed. Thus people make their baptismal promises again, even if no actual baptisms take place, and are sprinkled with the newly blessed water. The service continues in the usual form of a Eucharist. The Gloria, a hymn of praise, is sung for the first time since Ash Wednesday (apart from Maundy Thursday) and is especially joyful. The priest may sing the opening "Glory to God in the highest" and, before the people join in, the bells ring and the organ thunders (having been silent since early on Maundy Thursday evening). The word "Alleluia" is sung for the first time since the start of Lent. The whole service takes between one and two hours, and if it is a dawn service there is gradually increasing daylight to strengthen the symbolism of all the candles.

The Easter vigil is one of the most ancient services of the Christian Church, but churches which do not have such structural forms of worship may still hold a service at dawn, sometimes out of doors.

After the Easter service there is likely to be some form of party. If it is in the evening drinks may be served, or if early in the morning, breakfast. The services of Holy Week, particularly the ceremonies of Maundy Thursday and Good Friday, are likely to leave people feeling physically tired and emotionally drained but during the vigil the excitement gradually builds up, leaving them happy. Usually only a part of a church's

Metropolitan Trineos celebrates the Eucharist in Crete on Easter morning.

congregation will attend every service but by the end of the vigil the atmosphere can be one almost of relief at having weathered a crisis together.

In the morning there is at least one further celebration of the Eucharist, joyful again but without the ceremonies connected with the candle and the font. There is often an Easter garden: a model of a tomb in a garden of real (and usually disproportionately large) flowers, with three empty crosses above. Easter eggs symbolise new life, and the open egg is a reminder of the empty tomb. Orthodox Christians often crack hardboiled eggs against other people's eggs, saying "Christ is risen!".

See also *Candles, Eucharist, Resurrection, Lent, Holy Week.*

Ecumenism

It has been estimated that there are over 20,000 different sects or denominations within the whole Christian Church. Some are major groups (for example, roughly half the Christians in the world are Roman Catholics), others very small. In the twentieth century there has been a move to bring the various individual churches closer together. The name given to this movement is the "ecumenical movement". The word "ecumenical" comes from a Greek word meaning "the inhabited earth" or "the whole world". The intention is to show that despite disagreements the Christian Church is one throughout the world.

The Church of South India is one example of a group of churches joining together to resolve the bitternesses of the past. The Presbyterian, Methodist, Anglican and Congregational Churches of South India joined together in 1947 to share a common belief and to worship together.

In 1948 the World Council of Churches was formed. Its headquarters are in Geneva, Switzerland and it has member churches in many countries. The only major church that is not a member is the Roman Catholic Church though it has sent observers to the meetings since 1968. Among the 300 or so Christian groups belonging to the Council are Pentecostal, Orthodox, Anglican, Methodist, Baptist and United Reformed churches.

The importance of Christian Unity has been quite recently emphasized by the observance of a Week of Prayer for Christian Unity from 18-25 January each year. This is supported by the World Council of Churches and by the Vatican Secretariat

A Roman Catholic priest and a Baptist minister take part in a joint Eucharist as an act of unity. Notice that the bread and wine are still prepared in their separate ways, united in will but divided in action by the rules of their churches.

for Promoting Christian Unity. Perhaps it is worth noting that not all churches wish to promote unity. Some believe all the other churches are wrong – and even agents of the Devil. This means that the ecumenical ideal, that all Christians should be members of one church and able to worship together, although a worthy cause, may yet be a long way away in practice.

Eucharist

The Eucharist is very important for most Christians because it comes directly from a command of Jesus recorded in the Gospels. During supper on the night before he died he took some bread, gave thanks, broke it and distributed it to the disciples. He said, "This is my body which is given for you. Do this in memory of me." After supper he took a cup of wine and told them all to drink it. He said, "This cup is the new covenant in my blood, do this, whenever you drink it, in memory of me." During the Eucharist, therefore, bread and wine are blessed and shared.

There are great divisions between the churches over this service, but for most Christians it is an act which unites people with each other and with God, in which the sacrifice of Jesus's death is

remembered.

The service is usually in two parts. During the first part, sometimes called the Ministry of the Word, the Bible is read, a sermon is preached and prayers of intercession are said (see p. 50). Everyone may say a general "confession" and a "creed" (see p. 20 and p. 21). The first Christians were Jews and this part of the service bears some resemblance to synagogue services. It is followed by what is sometimes called the Ministry of the Sacrament, during which Jesus's words and actions at the Last Supper are repeated, and bread and wine are distributed. Churches with a strong liturgical tradition use patterns and even prayers which go back to the earliest known "liturgies" (see pp. 38-9). In these churches the Bible readings follow a two- or three-year plan and although there is some choice within the service it is only from a small group of prayers. Other churches give more freedom to the person leading the service, although in many cases there is some form of service book, particularly for the second part.

Many Christians believe that Christ is present in some way during the Eucharist. Some, such as Catholic and Orthodox Christians, believe that he is present in the consecrated bread and wine. They remain unchanged physically, but in a mysterious way *become* Christ's body and blood. The presence is objective and continues in any bread or wine not consumed. Jesus's death cannot be repeated, but it

The broken wafer held over the chalice containing ▷ wine is a powerful symbol in the Roman Catholic Church of Christ's sacrifice for all. The writing on the wafer is an abbreviation of the Greek word for Jesus. This sort of bread is "unleavened", that is, made without yeast.

The Last Supper is the meal upon which the Eucharist is based. In this picture Jesus is in the centre with John on his left and Peter on his right. Jesus holds a piece of bread towards Judas, who after receiving it goes out to betray him.

is made present. This is difficult to understand; it may be like a recording which can enable people to hear a concert from the past. Others believe that Christ is present when a believer receives the bread and wine in faith, but that they do not become holy in themselves.

Some Christians believe that the Last Supper was a Passover meal, and that the bread Jesus used was unleavened (made without yeast). The Passover recalls the Israelites' escape from slavery in Egypt. They left in a hurry and so made their bread without yeast because there was not time for it to rise. In most Catholic and Anglican churches, unleavened bread it used in the form of wafers which are like thin, white ice cream wafers, about the size of a two pence piece. Other churches, including the Orthodox Church, believe that the Last Supper was the night before the Passover, and so they use ordinary bread. Some non-conformist churches which discourage the drinking of alcohol use unfermented grape juice instead of wine.

People may move near the altar and stand or kneel to receive Holy Communion. Catholics usually receive just the bread; only the priest has bread and wine. In the Orthodox churches the bread is put into the wine and served on a spoon. In some non-conformist churches the bread and individual cups of wine are given to people in their places. Everyone then eats and drinks at the same time.

In Catholic, Anglican and Orthodox churches only priests and bishops may celebrate, or officiate at, the Eucharist. In most other churches it is usual for the minister to officiate, sometimes assisted by the elders or deacons, although some believe that others, usually men, may also do so.

There are several names for this service. "Eucharist" comes from the Greek word for "thanksgiving" and is widely used. Some non-conformist churches use the names "The Lord's Supper" or "The Breaking of Bread". Catholics often call it the "Mass". This is sometimes connected with the Latin words which end the service, "*Ite, missa est*", "Go, it is ended", but it seems odd to call a service after words of dismissal. Orthodox Christians call it the "Divine Liturgy" or "Holy Communion"; Holy Communion is a popular name for the service, used by many Christians.

The major Christian groups who do not hold this service are the Quakers and the Salvation Army.

See also *Bible (use)*, *Liturgy*, *Sacrament*.

Funeral

The way funerals are conducted varies from one denomination to another because Christians are divided over whether prayers should be offered for the dead. The early Christian Church inherited the Jewish custom of praying for the dead. Following the Reformation (see p. 13) some Protestant

After the service in church, the coffin is taken to be buried. Some of the mourners carry flowers which they will leave on the grave. This is the funeral of Dame Agatha Christie.

churches abandoned the practice because they believed that after death people would be judged by God according to the way they had lived; it would therefore be illogical to pray for them because it was too late to change anything.

The funeral of a believing Christian should be a joyful event, because he or she has gone to be with God. People may say that the dead person has "gone to glory". Some Christians include in their funeral services readings of hope and promise (e.g. John 14:1-6) but still pray for the dead person to be received into God's care and forgiven for his sins. Despite certain differences of belief, all Christians reject the idea of reincarnation. They believe rather that each person has a soul which comes into being with that person and which has not been nor ever will be part of anyone else.

On the day before a funeral a body may be received into a church, where it remains overnight. Otherwise the funeral begins with the body being taken into church, usually followed by the family, and met by the priest or minister at the door. The coffin rests on a stand or a table at the front of the church and may have candles placed around it and flowers on top, as symbols of the continued life of the soul, despite the death of the body. The funeral service contains readings about the Resurrection, as well as prayers which may thank God for the life of the person, commending him to God's mercy, and asking God to comfort those who mourn and help them to make the best use of the time that is left to them. Something may be said about the person's life, and a Eucharist (see p. 25) may be celebrated. This shows that the dead person is still part of the Christian Church. In remembering the death of Christ the living are asking God to bring the dead person to share in the eternal life which the death of Jesus brought about. This sort of Eucharist may also be celebrated after the funeral, when it is called a Requiem Mass (after the first word of the Latin service which means "Rest"). Relatives and friends may ask for a requiem to be said on the anniversary of a person's death, or if they have been unable to attend the funeral.

After the service in church the body is buried or cremated and there is a short service of commendation, either at the graveside or in the crematorium. If the body is cremated, or buried in a cemetary rather than a churchyard, the whole service may take place in the crematorium or cemetery chapel.

Many churches have special services for a child's funeral. The Anglican Alternative Services Book has also introduced prayers for the funeral of a newly born or still-born child; these are used in hospital chapels in particular.

Funerals usually take place within a few days of a person's death, unless there are unusual circumstances such as the cause of death being uncertain or the body being needed for police examination. The funeral may later be followed by a memorial service where the body is not present; for this there is no set form, although the service generally includes hymns, readings from the Bible and prayers. Memorial services are especially common when the dead person was a well-known national figure such as an actor or a politician. Frequently, a family will prefer to keep a funeral small and private; then many others can attend the memorial service.

See also *Death*.

God

Christians believe in one God who has revealed himself to the world as Father, Son and Holy Spirit. The relationship between Father, Son and Holy Spirit is mysterious and cannot be explained. These are *not* three gods, but different sorts of activity of God. The term Trinity is used to cover the activity of Father, Son and Holy Spirit – one God.

Generally, Christians believe that God has a close personal relationship with his creation. The terms "Father", "Son" and "Holy Spirit" give some guidance as to that very close personal contact: God as a loving Father, an obedient and loving Son and ever present in all of creation through the Holy Spirit. It is important to remember that the three members of the Trinity are one God and always act together; they cannot be conveniently separated out. That would appear to be making three separate gods.

Some Christian groups place particular emphasis on one member of the Trinity, perhaps Jesus Christ or the Holy Spirit, but Christians believe God has always existed as Trinity. "There was [a time] when he [Christ] was not" was judged a heresy by the early Christian Church. That God has revealed himself in many ways, particularly through the history of the people of Israel, its prophets and its teachings, and most completely in the person of Jesus of Nazareth, would be agreed by most Christians.

Trinity Sunday is a festival celebrated by some Christian churches on the Sunday after Pentecost.

It has been a festival since the tenth century C.E., celebrating the glory and majesty of God.

At baptism virtually all Christian churches use the formula. "I baptize you in the name of the Father and of the Son and of the Holy Spirit" (Matthew 28:19). The number 3 has significance in all aspects of Christianity as a means of remembering the Trinity; some Christians make the sign of the Cross when mentioning the Father, Son and Holy Spirit, particularly when they begin their prayers.

In art the Father is often represented by an elderly figure, the Son shown on the cross or a throne, and the Holy Spirit depicted as a dove (see Mark 1:10).

See also *Jesus, Pentecost*.

Grace

Christians recognize that while they may ask God for help they cannot *make* him do what they want. Whatever is given to each person is given by God who knows what is best. It is for God to decide how he answers the prayers offered to him. It is love of God, the personal response to each individual, that is called "grace". For most Christians, God revealed his grace most completely in the gift of his son Jesus. It was, Christians believe, through the life, death and resurrection of Jesus that salvation was made possible. A prayer often spoken by Christians at the end of prayers is "Not what I will but what you will", making it clear that God's will is of the greatest importance. Services or meetings often end with the "Grace" being said: "The grace of our Lord Jesus Christ and the love of God and the fellowship of the Holy Spirit be with us all." A more familiar use of the Grace is the prayer before meals when Christians ask God for a blessing, give thanks for the food and remember those who have nothing.

Holy Week

On Palm Sunday Christians remember Jesus riding into Jerusalem on a donkey while the people cheered, waved palm branches and shouted "Hosanna to the Son of David! Blessed is he who comes in the name of the Lord!". (See Matthew 21:1-11.) This was when Jesus' popularity was at its height, and the welcome that the people gave him may mean that they thought he would free them from the Romans.

Today, on Palm Sunday a procession may start from outside the church and finish inside, or begin and end inside the church but go outside, sometimes circling the building. Branches are often tied to the processional candles and cross, and the congregation may be given small palm crosses to hold. Recently, people have begun to carry whole branches of whatever grows locally. This part of the service may have something of the atmosphere of a carnival, but the mood changes quickly. During the Eucharist (see p. 25) the Gospel reading concerns the trial and crucifixion of Jesus; this is called the Passion. It is usually a very long reading and reminds people that Jesus went into Jerusalem triumphantly, but was crucified the same week. Crosses and crucifixes in the church may be covered.

On Monday, Tuesday and Wednesday in Holy Week there may be extra services in the evening with more long readings concerning the last days of Jesus' life. Thursday is called Maundy Thursday

An open air procession on Palm Sunday in Fiji. Notice the branches held by the servers and attached to the crucifix. Some of the people are carrying palm crosses.

Jesus washes Peter's feet at the Last Supper. ▷

and it is the day when the Last Supper, Jesus' prayer in the garden and his arrest are commemorated. "Maundy" comes from a Latin word "*mandatum*" meaning "command"; Jesus said to the disciples, "A new commandment [*mandatum novum*] I give to you, that you love one another even as I have loved you" (John 13:34). Jesus said this when he had washed the disciples' feet, and on this day the priest may begin the service by washing the feet of some members of the congregation. The Pope and other Christian leaders also wash people's feet. The giving of "Maundy money" by the Queen is a survival of a ceremony where the monarch used to perform a similar act. The point of such actions is that people should gladly perform kind acts for people of lower status. On the morning of Maundy Thursday it is traditional for Anglican and Catholic bishops to bless oils in their cathedrals. The oils are used throughout the year to anoint the sick, as well as in baptisms and confirmations.

In the evening of Maundy Thursday the Last Supper is remembered. In Anglican and Catholic

The crucifixion scene from the Passion Play at Oberammergau. The play has been performed every ten years since 1633 when the village was delivered from plague. It lasts about six hours and has a cast of about 700 villagers. It is performed many times in each season and is watched by people from all over the world.

churches there may be a fairly long service which begins joyfully. White vestments are worn, and the Gloria is sung for the first time since Ash Wednesday. At the Gloria the bells are rung, but then remain silent until Saturday evening. Extra bread is consecrated because it will be needed on Friday as well. After the communion there is a solemn procession and the extra consecrated bread is taken to a side chapel (the Lady Chapel if there is one). This is usually decorated with flowers and candles, because after the Last Supper the gospels record that Jesus went to a garden called Gethsemane to pray (Matthew 26:36). Jesus was in great agony because he did not want to die, and he prayed for a long time. The disciples fell asleep, even though Jesus had asked them to watch with him; when Jesus found them he said, "Could you not watch with me one hour?". People may try to "watch with Jesus" by spending some time in the chapel in silence. Sometimes a rota may be arranged so that the watch is continuous until midnight or occasionally throughout the night. Meanwhile all the coverings are removed from the altar, which is left bare and empty.

Good Friday is a solemn and sad day. The story of the trial and death of Jesus is read or sung, usually from St John's Gospel. In a ceremony called the Veneration of the Cross a veiled crucifix (see p. 22) is taken to a central place in the church and gradually uncovered. People may kiss it in turn, to show their love for Jesus. The Eucharist (see p. 25) is not celebrated on this day but some people may receive Holy Communion from the bread reserved from the previous evening. None is conserved on this occasion: the church is left without the sacramental presence of Christ until Easter is celebrated, as a sign that Jesus was dead and buried at this time. During this service the singing is often unaccompanied, the organ silent.

It is customary for many Christian churches to hold services between twelve and three o'clock in the afternoon – the time when Jesus was dying on the cross. There is no set form for these, but they usually include a series of talks, perhaps one every half hour, as well as hymns, prayers, readings and periods of silence. The composer J.S. Bach's great "Passions", *St John* and *St Matthew*, which combine the Biblical text with reflections and hymn-like "chorales" in a lengthy and elaborate musical setting, were originally written for the Lutheran church in Germany. Today they are frequently performed in both cathedrals and concert halls during Lent and on Good Friday. In this country it is customary that no matter where such performances take place their religious character is marked by the absence of applause, a distinction not given to any other concert hall performances of religious music.

Hot-cross buns are eaten on Good Friday. The cross stands for the cross on which Jesus died, while the spices in it are a reminder of the spices which Jews traditionally wrapped around bodies before burial (John 19:39).

See also *Easter, Jesus, Lent*.

Icon

An icon is a picture of Jesus, the Virgin Mary or another saint, usually painted on wood but sometimes created in another medium such as mosaic. Icons have a distinctive, formalized style and are most common in Orthodox churches, where they may be kissed and have candles burnt in front of them as a sign of respect. The screen which separates the sanctuary, where the altar is, from the central nave in Orthodox churches is called an "iconostasis" because it is covered in icons. It is believed that saints can exercise their powers through icons, and some have been famous for the miracles they are believed to have performed.

See also *Saint, Cross*.

Two Orthodox priests paint icons of St John the Baptist.

Incense

Incense is used by many religions, and at the time of Jesus it was burned in the Temple in Jerusalem. In the Book of Revelation there is a reference to angels in heaven burning incense; this may suggest that it was used in the earliest days of the Christian Church, but the evidence is inconclusive. Within the Christian Church it is burnt only in Catholic, Orthodox and a few Anglican churches.

Incense is made from the resin of trees, and appears to be made up of large brown crystals. The sticks of incense used in other religions are not used in Christian churches. When grains of incense are put on smouldering charcoal a sweet smelling smoke is produced as they evaporate. Incense is burnt in a metal "thurible" or "censer" which is like a dish with a perforated lid. It hangs from chains which pass through the lid so that it can be lifted without being removed completely. The charcoal is put in the bottom half, and incense spooned in as necessary. The smoke emerges through the holes in the lid.

Incense symbolizes prayers rising to God (Revelation 8:3). It is also a way of employing the sense of smell in the act of worship. Elaborate ceremonies are connected with its use, and both people and holy things may be "censed", that is, have the smoke directed to them. People who are not used to incense usually cough when they are exposed to it; this was unknown in ancient times and is possibly a psychological reaction to seeing smoke. One useful result of burning incense is the elimination of moths from church furnishings.

Grains of incense have been sprinkled on glowing charcoal in the base of this thurible, and they turn to smoke which escapes through holes in the lid. The thurible is ready for use.

Initiation

To some Christians a baby is a member of the Church at birth, for all creation is God's creation. However, in some churches the baby becomes a member of the Church only at baptism. In Roman Catholic and Anglican Churches the parents and godparents make promises on behalf of the baby and pledge to help the child understand the Christian faith. The baby may be several weeks or months old when baptized. Roman Catholic, Anglican and those Protestant churches which baptize babies sprinkle or pour water over the head of the child – often three times – and sometimes make the sign of the cross (see p. 22) on its forehead. This is also called "christening".

In the Russian Orthodox Church babies are baptized when they are eight days old; this was traditionally the day upon which Jesus would have been circumcized as a baby. All Orthodox babies will be totally immersed three times in the holy water in the font; once for the Trinity, once for the death of past sins and once for new life in Jesus.

The word "baptism" comes from a Greek word meaning "immersion", which is why some churches believe that the baptized child or adult should be totally immersed in water. As the person being baptized goes down into the water so sin dies and the Christian is symbolically washed clean by the water, rising to a new life in Christ.

The Baptist Churches baptize only believers, which means that they will not baptize a person until he or she is old enough to make a personal commitment of faith. This is often called "believers' baptism". Many Baptist churches have a pool built under the floor in which the baptism can take place; it will be empty and covered over when not in use. In some Baptist churches there

△ Young girls dressed as brides to symbolize purity prepare to take their First Communion. This is an important step for Catholics so it is marked with great ceremony.

are two sets of steps: those to be baptized go down into the water by one set and come out by the other set of steps. Although children are not baptized there is a ceremony of "infant dedication". Pentecostal churches also practise believers' baptism in much the same way. In some countries of the world believers' baptism will take place in rivers or pools outdoors. An early Christian document, *The Didache*, recommends baptism in "living" (i.e. running) water if at all possible.

For Roman Catholic children the next important event after baptism – which they may be too young to remember – is First Communion. This may take

A priest baptizes an infant by pouring water from the font over the child's head. ▽

The bishop places his hands on the head of this boy to confirm him. The boy has already made for himself the promises his parents and godparents made when he was baptized. In the Church of England he may now take Communion for the first time. ▽

place at eight or nine years of age. The young child will come into church, often at Easter time, carrying a candle and be able to receive Holy Communion even though confirmation will not happen for some years. Confirmation is the ritual in which an older person "confirms" the promises made on their behalf when younger. It is considered an important stage in the spiritual growth of members of the Roman Catholic Church. In the Orthodox Church the baby, having been baptised, will immediately be confirmed. A priest applies holy ointment ("chrism") to the baby and it may join in Holy Communion from that date onwards. Most other churches receive young people into full membership when they are in their

teens. In the Anglican and Roman Catholic Churches the local bishop confirms each person by placing his hands on his or her head. Anglicans are at this point able to receive communion for the first time. Methodists and other Protestant churches often hold a short ceremony – usually in the course of a service – when young people make their promises and are welcomed into full membership of the church. In the Baptist Church the elders and the minister lay their heads upon each young person and pray for them. The Salvation Army mark this stage in life by swearing in the young members as soldiers.

See also *Sacrament, Unction.*

Jesus

There are two aspects of the person of Jesus which must be considered; the first is the historical person and the second is the Christian perception of him.

Despite the dating of years "B.C." (Before Christ) and "A.D." (*Anno Domini*, Latin for "in the year of the Lord") Jesus was probably born in Palestine in the year 4 B.C.E. (The mistake arose because it was not until the sixth century that this method of dating was begun.) The main sources of the story of his life are the four gospels. These are not biographies, however, so they leave many gaps: for example, we know neither what Jesus looked like nor how he spent most of his time until he was about 30.

From the Gospels it seems that Jesus was born in Bethlehem but grew up in the home of Joseph and Mary in Nazareth. The country of Palestine was part of the Roman Empire, but when Jesus was born it was still ruled by a Jewish king called Herod; by the time Jesus grew up the Romans had installed one of their officials in the area called Judaea, in southern Palestine, which included Jerusalem.

Jesus's mother was a young woman called Mary. She married Joseph, who brought Jesus up, although he was not Jesus's father. Jesus did not have a human father but was conceived by Mary while she was a virgin (Luke 1:26-38; Matthew 1:18-25). The family was Jewish and Jesus grew up going to the synagogue, probably travelling to Jerusalem for religious festivals. The only story about Jesus's childhood concerns a visit to Jerusalem when he was 12 (Luke 2:41-52).

When Jesus was about 30 he was baptized in the River Jordan by his cousin, John the Baptist. John was preaching and calling on his listeners to change

A very early picture of Jesus from the catacombs in Rome.

their ways of life and turn to God, to prepare the way for God to save them through his Messiah or Saviour (Luke 3:1-20). This baptism was a symbolic washing away of sins, but it was not the same as other Christian baptisms. After Jesus had been baptized a voice from heaven said that he was God's dear son (Luke 3:21-22). Jesus then went into the desert and fasted, and was tempted to prove himself by turning stones to bread and jumping from a high place, and to gain worldly power by worshipping the devil. Throughout, Jesus resisted temptation (Luke 4:1-13).

After this, Jesus began his ministry of teaching

and healing and chose 12 men to help him (Luke 6:12-16). One of the important parts of the work of Jesus was the preparation of his followers for the coming of the Kingdom of Heaven. Some of his teaching brought him into conflict with the religious authorities of the time, particularly when he was discussing areas where the religious law seemed to him to fuss about details but miss the point (Mark 7:1-23). Jesus attracted crowds of people and performed miracles, as when he fed "five thousand men, beside women and children" from five loaves and two fishes (Matthew 14:15-21). This period of his life probably lasted for about three years.

The accounts of the last week in the life of Jesus, which are in all the Gospels, are broadly similar but differ in some ways. The version which follows is necessarily simplified.

It seems from the Gospels that his popularity was at its height when Jesus rode into Jerusalem on what we now call Palm Sunday. The people welcomed him as king and called him the Son of David (because they believed that the Saviour would be a descendant of King David). By the following Thursday his teaching had made the religious leaders so angry that they wanted to kill him. Judas Iscariot, one of the 12 disciples, offered to lead them to Jesus when he was away from the crowds. That evening Jesus shared a meal with the disciples, known as the Last Supper. Afterwards he prayed in a garden called Gethsemane, and in great distress accepted God's will.

Jesus was arrested and tried on a charge of blasphemy, because he called himself the Son of God and so claimed equality with God. Under Jewish law blasphemy was punishable by death. Because of the Roman occupation of Jerusalem the sentence had to be confirmed by the Roman governor, Pontius Pilate. He seems to have been reluctant to condemn Jesus but was afraid that if he didn't then a riot might occur, as Jerusalem was overflowing with pilgrims who had come for the Passover festival and had to be kept under control. Crucifixion was the Roman method of execution for people who were not Roman citizens and Jesus was crucified immediately at a place called Golgotha, between two thieves. He was buried the same afternoon.

On Sunday morning his friends found that the tomb was empty, and over the following 40 days Jesus was seen by many people before he went bodily to heaven.

The most important beliefs held by Christians about Jesus are that he was the Son of God, yet human, and that he fulfilled the hope of the Jews that God would send a saviour or Messiah to mankind. "Messiah" comes from the Hebrew word for "anointed" and means the same as the Greek word "Christ". (Christ is a title given to Jesus, not a surname.) Jesus was not the founder of what we call Christianity: this began centuries earlier in Judaism, the religion of the Jews. Christians believe that the death of Jesus enables them to be forgiven, and that through his resurrection they can enjoy everlasting life.

For all Christians, faith means a personal response to Jesus. This may occur dramatically in a moment of conversion – which a believer is likely to express as "asking Jesus into his heart". For other Christians there may not be a single moment at which they could say their lives had changed, but faith may develop gradually from a point they cannot remember. In many ways faith is like falling in love, which may happen almost instantly or take months or even years. All Christians agree that faith is a free response and is not forced by God. The following is a frequently quoted verse:

> Behold, I stand at the door and knock; if anyone hears my voice and opens the door, I will come in to him and eat with him, and he with me.
> (Revelation 3:20)

There is a famous painting by Holman Hunt in St Paul's Cathedral which shows Jesus knocking on a door to which there is no handle, because it can only be opened from within. The door represents someone's heart.

Christians are likely to talk of having a relationship with Jesus which they may develop through prayer, through reading the Bible or through the sacraments. Holy Communion (the Eucharist) is a sharing of the body and blood of Christ and many Christians feel conscious of his presence at this time.

Christians believe that one day the world as we know it will end, and then Jesus will be revealed as a glorious king, in great contrast to his humble birth in Bethlehem. The earliest Christians thought that this would happen within their own lifetimes, but the later New Testament writers postponed their hope to the indefinite future. Some groups still try to predict when the world will end but they are not within any of the mainstream churches. Most Christians see no point in speculation.

See also *Ascension, Christmas, Easter, Eucharist, Holy Week, John the Baptist, Joseph, Lent, Mary, Prayer.*

John the Baptist

John the Baptist is described in the Gospel of Mark as "living on locusts and wild honey" and to Christians he represents the end of one line of Old Testament prophecy. St Luke's Gospel (Chapter 1) tells the story of his conception and birth before that of Jesus (which occurred six months later). Luke even describes Elizabeth, John's mother as a kinswoman (relative) of Mary, mother of Jesus. Such emphasis on John – in all the Gospels – shows that the writers considered him to be the prophet whom some Jewish authorities said would precede the coming of the Messiah, Jesus.

Certainly, John was dedicated to God. His long hair and humble lifestyle may indicate that he was a Nazirite, a member of a particularly devout, though small, group of Jews. His mission, according to the Gospels, was to prepare the way for one who was greater. He called the people to repent of their evil ways and to return to the true worship of God:

> I baptize you with water, for repentance; but the one who comes after me is mightier than I, and I am not fit to take off his shoes; he will baptize you with the Holy Spirit and with fire.
> (Matthew 3:11)

John baptized people in the River Jordan in Galilee. Matthew's Gospel records how when Jesus came to John for baptism, John tried to dissuade him, saying "I need to be baptized by you", but Jesus silenced his objection. Then:

After baptism Jesus came up out of the water at once, and at that moment heaven opened; he saw the Spirit of God descending like a dove to alight upon him; and a voice from heaven was heard saying, "This is my Son, my Beloved, on whom my favour rests."
(Matthew 3:13-17)

John seems to have criticized King Herod (not the Herod that Matthew says tried to kill the baby Jesus) for immorality because Herod had married his brother's wife Herodias while his brother was still alive. John was imprisoned and later beheaded after the daughter of Herodias had danced and pleased Herod. He asked her what she would like and at her mother's suggestion the head of John the Baptist was brought to her (Mark 6:14-19).

Jesus is reported by Matthew to have said:

> I tell you this: never has there appeared on earth a mother's son greater than John the Baptist, and yet the least in the kingdom of Heaven is greater than he. . . . John is the destined Elijah [the prophet to precede the Messiah].
> (Matthew 11:11-15)

See also *Jesus, Saint.*

This painting by Piero della Francesco shows John ▷ the Baptist baptizing Jesus in the River Jordan. The Holy Spirit is shown as a dove, in accordance with the Gospel accounts.

Joseph

Joseph plays an important part in the stories of the birth of Christ because Mary was betrothed to him at the time when she conceived Jesus, although she was still a virgin and Joseph was not his natural father. In Matthew's Gospel there are accounts of three dreams which Joseph had. One told him not to be afraid to marry Mary after he had decided not to go ahead with the wedding as she was pregnant; the second told him to take the infant Jesus and Mary to Egypt because King Herod was trying to find the child to kill him, and the third told him when the king was dead and it was safe to return to Nazareth (Matthew 1:18-25 and 2:13-23).

Jesus was born in Bethlehem because Joseph was descended from King David. At this time the Roman government had ordered everyone to return to their home towns, and Bethlehem was the city of David. Jesus grew up in the house of Nazareth where Joseph was a carpenter. Nothing is told of Joseph in the New Testament after the stories of Jesus' childhood. Traditionally Joseph was believed to be quite old at the time of the birth of Jesus and it is assumed that he died before Jesus' period of teaching began.

Joseph is given an honoured position among the saints as the guardian or foster father of Jesus. His memory is celebrated on 19 March or 1 May, the latter being the feast-day of St Joseph the Worker.

See also *Mary, Saint.*

Lent

The day before Lent begins is called Shrove Tuesday, named after the old Christian practice of going to confession before Lent. The word "Shrove" comes from the Middle English word "shriven" which means to attend confession to receive absolution and penance. On Shrove Tuesday all fat used to be put out of the house; sometimes this could lead to a party like the "Mardi Gras" ("Fat Tuesday"). More common in Britain is the custom of making of pancakes.

Lent is the period of 40 days before Easter. It is a time of penance, a preparation for the happy celebration at Easter. Lent begins on Ash Wednesday, so called because in some churches Christians have their priests mark their foreheads with ash as a sign of penitence. The other reason for this is to show that the worshipper is only as ashes before God and totally dependent on Him. "Remember O man that dust thou art and to dust shalt thou return" are the words of the priest as he puts the ashes on the forehead of the worshipper.

In earlier centuries the period of Lent was a time when new candidates were prepared for baptism. They would be baptized at Easter to share in the feast of new life. During Lent many Christians will fast, although today this may be only a token gesture such as the giving up of chocolates. They may give money to charity, join study groups to prepare for Easter, or make a special effort with their prayers either in private or by going to additional prayer meetings and services at church.

See also *Confession, Easter, Holy Week*.

On Ash Wednesday many Christians have a cross marked in ash on their foreheads. This act begins a period of discipline and self-examination before the Easter celebration.

Liturgy

"Liturgy" is derived from two Greek words meaning "the work of the people" although before Christian times it had already been used to refer to services in the temple at Jerusalem. Worship is thus seen as the people's work. In the West the word is used of all the services of the Church which have a fixed form, whereas in the East it is used almost exclusively to mean the Eucharist.

Christian liturgy is as old as Christianity, and the

An Anglican priest faces the congregation at the beginning of the Eucharistic prayer. He is wearing a chasuble (see p. 57). Notice the curtain on the wall which covers an aumbry. The eagle on the right is a traditional reading desk or lectern which holds a Bible. It symbolizes the word of God being carried around the world.

pattern of the Eucharist in Anglican and Catholic churches, for example, can be traced back to at least the second century after Christ, although parts of it are of earlier Jewish origin. The first account of the Eucharist is in one of Paul's letters and some scholars believe that Paul was quoting part of a liturgy which had already been established, perhaps as early as 52 C.E. (I Corinthians 11:23-25).

Liturgy is important to Christians for several reasons. It represents the beliefs of the Church as a whole and not just the person taking the service; it is the same in all churches of one denomination and unites the different congregations. Christians know that if they are away and go to church they will take part in a service with which they are familiar. The liturgy also unites them with Christians of the past who attended the same services. Liturgy is the result of centuries of Christian prayer and reflection and has produced beautiful images on which the worshipper can meditate; repetition leads to a familiarity with the words which allows the worshipper to pray whole-heartedly because he is not distracted by them.

See also *Eucharist, Prayer Books*.

Marriage

The Christian view of marriage varies slightly from church to church. The Gospels teach that marriage is for life: divorce or re-marriage is not allowed. However, in Matthew's Gospel it does appear that adultery or "unchastity", as it is called, is a possible reason for divorce (Matthew 5:32). The New Testament depicts marriage as an image of the relationship between Christ and his church in which both partners love and are loved unselfishly.

Many couples marry in church; some will be practising Christians, others not. For those who are it is a special celebration in which the two partners pledge to live together forever in the presence of God. Sometimes this is marked by a Mass or Eucharist celebrated during the service. The clergyman marrying the couple will normally have met them several times to talk about the arrangements for the day and, more importantly, to help prepare the couple for their life together.

Generally speaking, the Christian argument against divorce is that if a couple promise to accept the responsiblity of marriage before God then they cannot be released from that vow, as it is taken for life. A couple may have a civil (non-religious) divorce and marry again, but within some churches – the Roman Catholic Church in particular – neither the divorce nor the re-marriage will be recognized and the divorced person will be considered to be living in adultery. A marriage can be declared "null and void" by the Roman Catholic Church but this requires a special "dispensation" and is quite rare. It means that the marriage is regarded as never having taken place.

Some of the Free or Non-Conformist churches and the Reformed churches allow re-marriage. The Church of England does not favour divorce although an Anglican priest can perform a re-marriage if one of the partners lives in his parish and he is willing. The old language of the marriage

Many Christian couples begin their married life with a Eucharist celebrated immediately after the wedding ceremony. Here the bride receives the chalice.

ceremony "those whom God has joined together let no man put asunder [apart]" – sums up the traditional approach of the Church to the matter, although in societies where divorce is more common it is more sympathetic to those involved in a distressing marriage break-up.

See also *Eucharist, Sacrament*.

Mary

Mary is a central figure in Christianity because it was through her that God became incarnate (made flesh). She is often called the "Blessed Virgin Mary" because Christians believe that when Jesus was conceived Mary was still a virgin, and thus that he did not have a human father. At this time Mary was promised in marriage to Joseph, who married her in spite of his initial doubts, bringing up Jesus as his own son.

Mary is mentioned in several Biblical stories: in that of the wedding at Cana she asks Jesus for his help because the wine has run out (John 2:1-11); at another point, when his mother and brothers want to speak to him, Jesus pays Mary less attention, saying that everyone who does as God wishes is his mother and brother (Mark 3:31-35). Nevertheless, Mary was at the cross when Jesus was crucified, and he gave her into the care of John, his beloved disciple (John 20:25-27). This adds weight to the belief that Joseph had died by then. After the Ascension Mary remained in Jerusalem with the disciples, where they "devoted themselves to prayer" (Acts 1:14). This is the last mention of Mary in the New Testament.

One ancient tradition relates that Mary's parents were called Anna and Joachim and that they were old when she was born. Roman Catholics believe that Mary was born without "original sin" – the stain of sin which has affected everyone since Adam and Eve. This birth is known as the "Immaculate Conception", and should not be confused with the "Virgin Birth" which refers to the fact that Mary was a virgin when Jesus was conceived. From the fourth century C.E. onwards some Christians have believed that after her death Mary's body was taken to heaven. This is known as the "Assumption", after which Mary was crowned as the Queen of Heaven.

Mary has several feast-days: those deriving from the New Testament are the Annunciation (Luke 1:26-38) on 21 March; the visit to Elizabeth (Luke 1:39-56) on 2 July or 31 May, and the presentation of Jesus in the Temple (Luke 2:22-40) on 2 February, also called Candlemas. Other related festivals include the Immaculate Conception (8 December), Mary's birthday (8 September) and the Assumption (15 August).

Many Christians, particularly Roman Catholic and Orthodox Christians, have a special devotion to Mary, but although they pay her honour it falls short of the worship given to God. One of the most popular prayers for such believers is the "Hail Mary". The beginning is a combination of the

Statues of Mary are commonly found in Catholic churches and may appear elsewhere. This statue shows Mary with a circle of 12 stars around her head, in accordance with a passage in Revelation 12.

angel's greeting to Mary at the Annunciation and Elizabeth's greeting when Mary visited her:

Hail Mary, full of grace, the Lord is with thee; blessed art thou among women and blessed is the fruit of thy womb, Jesus. Holy Mary, Mother of God, pray for us sinners now and at the hour of our death.

Some Christians believe that they can ask the saints in heaven to pray for them, just as they can ask friends on earth to pray.

At times, devotion to Mary has become so widespread and fervent that it has seemed as though she was being treated as a sort of goddess. As a result, many Protestants believe nothing about her beyond what is written in the New Testament. They do not ask Mary or any other saints to pray for them, but address their prayers directly to God.

The earliest recorded vision of the Blessed Virgin Mary occurred in the third century C.E. Two of the most famous visions in recent times occurred at Lourdes, in France (where Bernadette, under Mary's direction, discovered a spring whch is believed to have healing powers) and at Fatima, in Portugal, where three children saw "Our Lady of the Rosary" in 1917. In England there is a shrine of Our Lady at Walsingham.

See also *Jesus, Joseph, Saint.*

Meditation

Meditation is the concentration of the mind upon a particular thing. Some Christians meditate a great deal, and some religious orders of nuns and monks are "contemplative", which means that they see prayer as their principal aim although they earn their keep through manual work. There are different methods of meditation but it usually involves sitting or kneeling and concentrating upon one aspect of the life of Jesus – often his crucifixion. Some might concentrate upon the poor or the suffering; others might repeat the name of Jesus, or Mary his mother, or recite short prayers.

The most common aid to meditation is probably the crucifix – the image of Jesus hanging on the cross. However, many Roman Catholics, Orthodox and Anglican Christians will use a rosary to help them. A rosary is a set of beads with a crucifix attached, which the worshipper uses to "count off" prayers.

See also *Prayer, Rosary.*

Missionary

Full authority in heaven and on earth has been committed to me. Go forth therefore and make all nations my disciples; baptize men everywhere in the name of the Father and the Son and the Holy Spirit, and teach them to observe all that I have commanded you. And be assured I am with you always, to the end of time.
(Matthew 28:18-20)

During the 1930s in Canada, missionaries would use a van to visit outlying farms. It contained a bed and food and served as a travelling mission station.

Matthew's Gospel ends with these words, which together with other Gospel passages (Luke 10:1-24; Luke 9:1-6; Matthew 10:1-11), provide a firm basis for Christians to go into the world teaching and preaching about the life and work of Jesus. Such people are called "missionaries" because they believe God has given them a mission to preach the Gospel to those who do not believe, or have not heard it. The word "evangelist" is from the Greek meaning "good news"; an evangelist preaches the good news of the Gospel either to those new to Christianity or to those who already believe it. The writers of the four Gospels are sometimes called evangelists because they wrote about the good news.

Christianity is a missionary religion in the sense that the Church has always believed that the life and teaching of Jesus should be made known to all people in the world. It encourages religious conversion, and missionaries are active in many countries of the world. Some missionaries are doctors or nurses who combine their missionary activities with healing and medical care. However, many Christians working in a mainly non-Christian society believe that the most effective method of evangelism is simply to lead a devout Christian life. In other words they may not openly preach the Gospel but believe that their example of love and faith will bear witness to their devotion. In this way they may draw others closer to what they believe.

The eighteenth, nineteenth and twentieth centuries have seen missionary activity on a huge scale in India, Africa, South America and the Far East. The Church Missionary Society is a major organization supporting evangelists in every part of the world.

Morality

The basis of Christian morality is found in the Old Testament, to which the Commandments form a guide, as does the Torah – the first five books of the Bible. Most of the ethical teaching of Jesus has strong roots in the Old Testament or in the teaching of contemporary Jewish traditions. In fact modern Jewish scholarship has suggested that all of his teaching derived from Jewish sources. This is not surprising of course, for Jesus was a Jew and it would be natural for him to teach in the same manner as his contemporaries.

The main body of Christ's ethical teaching is found in the Sermon on the Mount (Matthew Chapters 5-8). It is echoed in Luke's Gospel (6:17-49) often called the Sermon on the Plain. In these many examples are given of how Christians should live: they should be prepared to give up everything to follow Jesus; they should take no thoughts for their needs for God will provide; they should turn the other cheek if provoked, and so on.

Christ's teaching is summed up in the words of the lawyer in Luke 10:25-28:

How difficult and lonely it can be to make moral decisions. This cartoon was drawn by a Quaker who was a conscientious objector imprisoned during the First World War.

On one occasion a lawyer came forward to put a test question to him: "Master, what must I do to inherit eternal life?" Jesus said, "What is written in the Law? What is your reading of it?" He replied, "Love the Lord your God with all your heart, with all your soul, with all your strength, and with all your mind; and your neighbour as yourself." "That is the right answer", said Jesus; "do that and you will live".

The Epistles contain many warnings about falling into bad ways. Drinking, adultery, lying, evil behaviour and indecency are all part of Paul's concern for the churches to which he wrote. Paul says that the fight of Christians is not against human foes but against evil:

In a word, as God's dear children, try to be like him, and live in love as Christ loved you, and gave himself up on your behalf as an offering and sacrifice whose fragrance is pleasing to God. (Ephesians 5:1-2)

He added

Stand firm, I say. Buckle on the belt of truth, for coat of mail put on integrity; let the shoes on your feet be the gospel of peace, to give you firm footing.
(Ephesians 6:14-15)

As the history of the Church unfolded over 2000 years, certain social and moral issues arose which were not specifically mentioned in the New Testament. Also, changes in society meant that some Christians felt that the Church had to interpret the teachings of Jesus in the light of the times in which they lived. Thus while Christian teaching has always been very clear concerning, for example, sexual relationships before or outside marriage, the various churches have had to consider how they respond to those who break the rule but still wish to worship in church and practise their Christian faith. This may be most clearly seen in the cases of marriage, divorce, abortion and contraception where the different churches hold differing opinions.

Some Christians fight injustice as part of their belief in God. Desmond Tutu, the black Anglican archbishop of Cape Town, is outspoken in his opposition to apartheid. He believes that the discrimination between black and white people enforced by the South African government is fundamentally immoral and opposed to all Christian ethical and moral principles. Camillo Torres, a Roman Catholic priest in Columbia, was forced to leave the church because of his involvement with revolutionary guerilla movements. He believed that revolution was the only way to improve the life of the poor, and saw it, therefore, as a Christian act of love.

Sometimes situations arise for which there is no direct guidance from the Bible or from the traditional teaching of the Church. This is particularly the case with medical and scientific questions, such as how should Christians respond to "*in vitro* fertilization" of an ovum (producing test tube babies). In such circumstances Christians must be guided by what they themselves believe about the nature of God, the value of human life and the sanctity of marriage.

See also *Authority, Bible (use), Commandments*.

Music

Music has an important role in most Christian churches. Choirs have been known since the fourth century C.E.; in many churches a choir leads the singing of the congregation and may sing alone at certain points during the service. In most churches the choir is drawn from among the congregation but many cathedrals have professional choristers, usually male – either men from the area or boys educated at the cathedral's own school, where music tuition and practice are an important part of the school day. With this training even young boys reach a high degree of competence, and music of an excellent calibre is produced. The music of cathedral worship is very elaborate, and the congregation has little chance to participate in the singing. They may still worship, however, as the choir sings on their behalf rather than to them. This arrangement is normal in the Orthodox churches, where most of the singing is by the priest and choir.

In most churches in Europe there is an organ. This has been the custom since the Middle Ages although organs were outlawed in Britain for short periods under Puritan influence. An organ is ideal for use in a large building because it is versatile and can support the singing of a large congregation with just one person playing it. The Orthodox Church has maintained the tradition of the early Church in which all singing was unaccompanied. Some western churches omit the organ pieces which normally precede and follow services (known as "voluntaries") during the penitential seasons of Lent and Advent.

The only major Christian group whose worship excludes music is the Society of Friends. Elsewhere in the West the most common form of congregational singing is that of hymns, songs written in verses. The tradition of hymn singing is particularly strong in the non-conformist churches. One of the most famous writers of hymns was Charles Wesley whose works are sung not only by the Methodists who echo his beliefs but also by many other Christians. General Booth, who founded the Salvation Army, wrote many rousing hymns because, he said, "Why should the devil have all the best tunes?". In the Salvation Army, hymn singers are accompanied by a brass band, which can also play outside. Many evangelical and Roman Catholic churches have at least some services where guitars are used, often for hymns

which resemble folk songs. Like brass bands, guitars are easily moveable and suitable for meetings outside church buildings.

The choir of Westminster Abbey practises in the Abbey. Their dress is traditional.

Carols were originally songs for dancing, and reflected popular belief, in contrast to hymns which were written by people of more education. Carols were not sung in church. Today no distinction is made between hymns and carols, both of which are sung inside and outside churches. Carols are associated mostly with Christmas, although there are some connected with Advent and Easter.

Orthodox churches

See *Bible (use)*, *Church (history)*, *Creed*, *Eucharist*, *Icon*.

Parable

A parable is a particular form of teaching used by Jesus. It has been called an "earthly story with a heavenly meaning" but this is too simple a definition. Usually taking the form of a story, the parable is a way of helping the hearers to remember the main point, or else search for other relevant points. Most of the parables are ways of illustrating the teaching of Jesus about the Kingdom of God.

Some parables are quite long such as the Parable of the Sower (Mark 4:3-9) with its explanation (Mark 4:13-20), the Parable of the Good Samaritan (Luke 10:30-36) and the Parable of the Ruler and the Debtor (Mark 18:23-35). Others are very short, such as the Parable of the Mustard Seed (Mark 13:31-32), the Parable of the Pearl of Great Price (Mark 13:45-46), the Parable of the Yeast (Luke 13:20-21).

Some parables seem to have layers of meanings allowing the hearer to take something from them and then see further meanings as faith grows. It is thought by certain scholars that some of the parables may have been originally spoken by Jesus in a different context to that in which they appear in the Gospels. When we tell a story the meaning

撒馬利亞人行仁
図聖路加十章卅節

The parable of the Good Samaritan has universal appeal, as seen in this drawing from China.

may be slightly different depending upon to whom we tell it and where. It seems certain that Jesus used parables to teach, just as did most other Jewish teachers of his time, but readers in the twentieth century cannot always be sure of his original meaning.

Patron

Many churches have a patron saint, after whom they are called. Originally this was because churches were built over the tombs of martyrs (see p. 55). One of the best examples of this is the great cathedral of St Peter in the Vatican, built on the tomb of St Peter the Apostle. Patron saints are believed to pray for their particular causes in heaven and a church associated with a particular saint will celebrate the festival as one of the most important days in the year.

Some saints are associated with a particular trade or profession; for example, St Luke, who is believed to have been a doctor himself, is the patron saint of doctors. Countries often have patron saints: St George for England, St David for Wales, St Andrew for Scotland and St Patrick for Ireland all have some connection, however legendary, with the country concerned.

There are also saints associated with particular circumstances: Christopher is the patron saint of travellers, and Jude that of lost or desperate causes. Some Christians, particularly Catholics, regard any saint after whom they are named as their patron and they will try to copy that saint's particular characteristics. At confirmation or ordination people may take an extra name; this is usually that of a saint whom they particularly admire.

See also *Saint*.

Paul

Paul was known by his Jewish name of Saul before his conversion on the road to Damascus when he decided to follow Jesus. He was born of a Jewish family in Tarsus, a city in Cilicia (now part of Turkey) which meant that he could claim Roman citizenship, a great honour in the Roman Empire. He was trained as a rabbi in Jerusalem under the well known scholar, Gamaliel. At first he strongly opposed the followers of Jesus, trying to persecute and kill them. The Acts of the Apostles record that Paul was present at the death of Stephen, the first Christian martyr (Acts 8:1). In his letter to the Christian in Galatia he writes:

> . . . the gospel you heard me preach is no human invention. I did not take it from any man; no man taught it me; I received it through a revelation of Jesus Christ. You have heard what my manner of life was when I was still a practising Jew: how savagely I persecuted the Church of God and tried to destroy it. . . . But then in his good pleasure God . . . chose to reveal his Son to me and through me, in order that I may proclaim him among the Gentiles [non-Jews].
> (Galatians 1:11-16; see also Acts 9:1-30)

Paul's revelation (or conversion) occurred in about 33-4 C.E. (two years or so after the death of Jesus) and he then spent 14 years thinking deeply about the meaning of his conversion before meeting the followers of Jesus in Jerusalem. His conversion is commemorated on 25 January.

Paul became the leading apostle of the Christians, especially among the Gentiles. Most of his teaching is contained in letters he wrote to the churches in cities he visited. The New Testament contains 13 letters that bear his name, of which some were clearly written by other people but most are believed to be genuine. Paul made three great missionary journeys, to what are now Cyprus, Turkey and Greece. These are recounted in the Acts of the Apostles. He believed that the life, death and resurrection of Jesus had abolished all barriers between Jews and Gentiles. Gentiles who became Christians did not have to become Jews first, he argued, nor did Christians – whether Jewish or Gentile – have to follow Jewish religious and dietary laws. This caused tensions between him and some other Jewish Christians – notably Peter (see Galatians 2:11-14).

Paul continued to visit Jerusalem to maintain contact with the Church there until he was arrested on a charge of violating the temple. As a Roman citizen he could appeal to be tried in Rome, and he was sent there in about 59 C.E. It is uncertain what happened to him then: one tradition says he was released and later visited Spain and other parts of the Mediterranean; another says that after being held in Rome for two years, where he was able to preach, Paul was executed on the Osian Way near Rome.

The Roman Catholic Church celebrates Paul on 29 June, the same day as it celebrates Peter. These two are considered to be the twin founders of the Church. Paul is often called the formulator or shaper of the Christian Church because of his insistence upon the salvation offered to all mankind through Jesus. This can be seen in his letters to Rome, Corinth, Galatia, Ephesus and Thessalonica in particular.

See also *Jesus, Missionary, Saint*.

Pentecost

Pentecost is when Christians celebrate the coming of the Holy Spirit. This happened 50 days after Easter, ten days after the ascension of Jesus. "Pentecost" is the Greek name for a Jewish festival which occurs 50 days after Passover. The book of Acts says that on the day of Pentecost the disciples were in Jerusalem, gathered together in a house. A sound like the rushing of a wind was heard and tongues of flame descended on all of them and they suddenly found that they could speak many different languages (Acts 2:1-4). The Holy Spirit is often represented as breath or wind, illustrating the mysterious activity of God on earth, unseen yet causing change in people, just as when the wind blows a tree you cannot see the wind itself but you can see the branches moving. The Holy Spirit is also represented as fire, indicating enormous power.

Pentecost is sometimes called "Whitsun" or "Whit Sunday". This is because it used to be the second main time of the year for baptisms – Easter was the main occasion – and "Whit" comes from "white", referring to the white clothes that the newly-baptized wore. Most people would be surprised that Pentecost is officially the second most important festival of the Christian Church. Christmas and Easter are both celebrated with special services and various traditions, both in church and at home, whereas in Britain Pentecost no longer merits even a bank holiday. The event celebrated at Pentecost is important, however, because Christians believe that the Holy Spirit is the power of God working in them and in the world, without whom there would be no Church. Pentecost is sometimes called "the birthday of the Church".

See also *Ascension, Charismatic*.

A party of Pentecostal Christians pray in Jerusalem at what some Christians believe to be the tomb of Jesus.

Pentecostal churches

See *Charismatic, Church (history), Ecumenism, Initiation, Pentecost*.

Peter

Originally called Simon, Peter accepted his change of name when Jesus told him that he was the rock on which he would build his church. "Peter" comes from a Greek word meaning "rock" (Matthew 16:18-19). Before becoming a disciple of Jesus he was a fisherman by the Sea of Galilee; there are a number of references in the Gospel to the disciples fishing. Peter, with Andrew his brother, was fishing when "Jesus said to them, 'Come with me and I will make you fishers of men.' They left their nets at once and followed him" (Matthew 4:19-20)

Peter himself appears in the Gospels as rather impetuous but devoted to Jesus. It is often he who asks questions: "Lord, how often am I to forgive my brother if he goes on wronging me?" (Matthew 18:21; see also Matthew 19:27 and 15:15). It is he who is the first disciple to recognise Jesus as the Messiah (Mark 8:31; Matthew 16:15-16). Peter walks towards Jesus on water and as his faith reduces so he begins to sink (Matthew 14:28-33). He swears he will never disown Jesus even if

everyone else does (Mark 14:29) but fulfils Jesus' prophecy and denies him three times (Mark 14:66-72).

We know Peter was married because Jesus heals his mother-in-law (Matthew 8:14). Indeed he may have returned home for a time after the ascension of Jesus. He came to believe that Christ's teaching should not be reserved for the Jews alone, and had a vision (Acts 10:9-16 and 11:5-17) which persuaded him that "God has no favourites but that in every nation the man who is god-fearing and does what is right is acceptable to him" (Acts 10:34-36).

After the death of Jesus, Peter led the Jerusalem church for 20 years before moving to the eastern Mediterranean and ultimately to Rome. He was probably killed during the persecutions of Nero in about 62 C.E.; some traditions say that he was crucified upside down – at his own request – because he did not wish to die in the same way as Jesus.

Peter is considered to have been the first Bishop

of Rome, and the Roman Catholic Church regards him as the first in the succession of Popes claiming direct authority from Jesus.

During his time in Rome it is thought that Peter may have told his story of the life of Jesus to Mark, who then wrote his Gospel based on Peter's memories. Whatever the truth of this, the history of the Christian Church – and the Roman Catholic Church in particular – takes the following words of Jesus to Peter as being of great importance because of the authority behind them:

You are Peter, the Rock; and on this rock I will build my church and the forces of death shall never overpower it. I will give you the keys of the Kingdom of Heaven; what you forbid on earth shall be forbidden in heaven, and what you allow on earth shall be allowed in heaven. (Matthew 16:18-20)

See also *Authority, Jesus, Patron, Saint.*

Pilgrimage

A pilgrimage is a journey to a place which for some reason is considered holy. In Christian terms such places include those where Jesus lived or which he visited, and those where saints had visions or are buried. The motive of the pilgrim may be to make special prayers, to give thanks or to perform an act of repentance. In medieval times people would often have had a long and hazardous journey, but modern pilgrims usually travel by coach or even aeroplane.

There are many centres of pilgrimage in Israel, where Jesus lived. They are visited throughout the year, but especially at Christmas and Easter when people like to join celebrations in Bethlehem or Jerusalem. For example, on Good Friday people walk the route Jesus is believed to have walked to the place where he was crucified, and some carry a cross as Jesus did.

Many pilgrims visit Rome each year. St Peter is buried in the cathedral which bears his name and is important especially for Roman Catholics because the Pope is his successor as Bishop of Rome. People also go to Assisi, home of St Francis, and in 1986 it was here that the Pope, the Archbishop of Canterbury and leaders of other religions met to pray for peace in the world.

Pilgrimages are sometimes made to pray for healing. At Lourdes, in France, St Bernadette,

A group of pilgrims in St Peter's Square in Rome join the Pope in praying for peace.

The Bishop of Bath and Wells leads a procession from the parish church to the ruins of the old abbey in Glastonbury, Somerset. Thousands of Christians gather there on a Saturday in June each year.

This statue of Our Lady of Walsingham is based on a medieval seal, and was reconstructed when the shrine was revived this century. Mary carries a lily, which is a symbol of purity.

then a 14-year-old peasant girl, had a series of visions of the Virgin Mary in 1858. A spring of water appeared and miraculous healings are believed to have taken place there since 1873. Millions of pilgrims have made the journey to Lourdes, and although only a tiny proportion have been healed, many have found that their pilgrimage gives them a sense of peace. A similar shrine in England is at Walsingham in Norfolk. It was founded in the eleventh century by the Lady Richeldis who had a vision of the Virgin Mary and was told to build a copy of the house of Jesus in Nazareth. A well there is believed to have healing properties like the spring at Lourdes. The English shrine was destroyed during the Reformation in the sixteenth century, but was refounded in this century and is visited by Anglicans and Catholics alike.

See also *Easter, Mary, Saint*.

Prayer

The best known and probably most frequently used Christian prayer is the Lord's Prayer, sometimes called the Family Prayer or the "Our Father" (from the Latin "*Paternoster*"). It is the prayer which the Gospels record that Jesus taught his disciples when they asked him how they should pray (Luke 11:1-4; also see the version in Matthew 6:9-13). The version below is based on the text in the Gospels of Matthew and Luke. The last sentence is commonly added:

> Our Father in heaven, hallowed be your name. your kingdom come, your will be done, on earth as in heaven. Give us today our daily bread. Forgive us our sins as we forgive those who sin against us. Lead us not into temptation but deliver us from evil. For the kingdom, the power and the glory are yours, now and for ever. Amen.

This prayer has been a model for Christians from all denominations throughout the centuries.

There are many different types of Christian prayer. Some are concerned with praising God, adoring him for his grace and creation. Others are prayers of thanksgiving, said either from personal reasons or because God has bestowed his gifts upon the world. "Intercessory" prayers are made when the person or persons praying want to ask God for something for someone else. In some churches – generally Roman Catholic, Orthodox or Anglican – prayers may be offered to the saints in heaven or to the Virgin Mary, asking them to intercede on behalf of the one praying. People may pray about health, personal problems, famine, disease, war or separation, in fact about any issue that troubles them. It is always recognized that God's will should be done and that while God hears a prayer

he does not necessarily answer it by solving all problems. He is not an immediate granter of wishes.

In the three traditions mentioned above many prayers are centuries old, and their use in worship is set. The Protestant Churches place greater emphasis on "free prayer" where the minister will pray and members of the congregation join in. It is through prayer that all Christians believe they are able to develop a deeper personal relationship with God.

Many Christians kneel to pray, putting their hands together and bowing their heads, but others stand or sit. Some make the sign of the cross to remind them of the crucifixion of Jesus. Just as there is no set position for prayer so there is no set time, although many give a prayer of thanks, called "grace", before a meal. Christians pray at night before they go to sleep, and in the morning. There are various aids to prayer: the Rosary (see p. 54) is very common among Roman Catholic, Orthodox and some Anglican believers; Orthodox Christians may pray before an icon (see p. 31) while others may use a cross (more common in the Protestant Church) or a crucifix.

Prayers often finish with the "Gloria" and the word "Amen", meaning "so be it".

> Glory be to the Father and to the Son and to the Holy Spirit as it was in the beginning, is now and ever shall be, world without end. Amen.

Some people pray together in silence, either at regular church services or at special prayer meetings. Personal prayer is normally silent.

See also *Grace, Meditation, Prayer Books, Rosary.*

Prayer books

There are many books of prayers and services, some of which are for public worship while others are for people to use on their own at home. Churches which have fixed orders of services produce their own prayer books or service books. It takes a long time to agree upon and publish new services, so this is not done very often. There has been a great deal of activity in this area in recent years, however, leading to the publication of new Roman Catholic books in 1970 and 1971 and a new Anglican book, the first since 1662, in 1980. The books may be called prayer books or service books

if they are used for a variety of services. The Roman Catholic Church uses the name "missal" for a mass book and "breviary" for the book for offices (prayer through the day).

Prayer books may seem complicated because although most services follow a fixed pattern there are certain parts which vary. Thus, to follow a whole service the congregation may need to find two or three places in their books and know when to turn from one to another. For example, the readings from the Bible at the Eucharist (see p. 25) change daily or weekly; some churches print a list

Prayer is not restricted by age or culture, but is universal.

of pages each week to help people who are not familiar with the book to find their way around.

There are several reasons for using prayer books: they unite the members of a particular church who all use the same services; they reflect the beliefs of the denomination as a whole, not of the person who is leading the service; and, moreover, Christians who are familiar with this sort of worship often find that because they know what is happening (and frequently know much of the service by heart) they are able to worship with more concentration, without the distraction of wondering what will happen next. People who say the offices from a breviary often do so alone and yet they know that others all over the world are doing the same, so they feel part of a community.

Many books of prayer are published commercially and used by people at home. The prayers may be classics, written many centuries ago but still used and found helpful, or they may be more recent. Prayers are often written for a particular group of people such as children or families, or for particular circumstances such as when someone has died or when going to receive Holy Communion. People find such books helpful when they want to pray but either do not know how to or perhaps are too upset to think of words for themselves. Christians believe that it is the thought behind the prayer which is important, so it does not matter whether the prayer has been written by someone else or has been made up – as long as it is sincerely meant.

See also *Liturgy, Prayer.*

Preaching

One of the fundamental aspects of Christian worship is the preaching of the Word of God. John's Gospel refers to Jesus himself as the "Word" (John 1:1-4) and preaching based on a scripture has become a very powerful method of spreading the Christian faith. Jesus himself taught, the best known section in the Gospels probably being his Sermon on the Mount (Matthew Chapters 5-7), and the apostles followed his example.

Most churches have a sermon or an address during a service, although the length of this may vary. The sermon will usually explain a text from the Bible, making a point about Christian belief and practice. Some churches, such as the Methodist Church, were – and remain – famous for the quality and length of their sermons based upon a particular Bible text. The tradition of preaching in the Roman Catholic Church is, generally speaking, not as strong; the sermon here is usually a brief homily rather than an extended address.

See also *Bible (use), Liturgy.*

A young priest preaches a sermon in an Orthodox church in Moscow. Notice that the congregation are standing and have gathered closely around him.

Protestant churches

See *Authority, Bible (use), Church (history), Church (organization), Eucharist.*

Repentance

John the Baptist called for all men to "repent", and this has become an integral part of the Christian faith. The idea of repentance involves a change: one must change one's ways or be sorry for one's actions allowing a real change might occur. For some Christians repentance is a once-and-for-all change; afterwards one lives in the Kingdom of God.

Repentance is expressed through confession in some churches, but in others it depends more upon the personal and direct relationship of a believer with God, as in the Protestant churches. In all churches there are services containing prayers which invite the worshippers to remember and reflect upon their selfish ways, asking for God's forgiveness and guidance to lead a better life.

See also *Confession, Jesus, Salvation, Sin.*

Resurrection

It is a fundamental belief of all Christians that Jesus died, was buried, and on the third day was raised to life. St Paul says:

> For I delivered to you as of first importance that Christ died for our sins, that he was buried, that he was raised on the third day in accordance with the scriptures, and that he appeared to Cephas [Peter], then to the twelve.
> (I Corinthians 15:3)

Paul does not speak of Jesus "dying and being seen", which might mean that his followers saw him just in visions, but says that he was buried and was *raised*, indicating that more definite events took place. Paul's account was written before any of the Gospels, which give fuller descriptions of these events.

After Christ's crucifixion on Good Friday he was buried in a tomb. Saturday is the Jewish sabbath, so his friends rested in accordance with the law, and it was Sunday morning before anyone went back to where Jesus was buried. Mary Magdalene and other women found the stone rolled away from the entrance and the body of Jesus gone. According to Matthew, the tomb had been guarded by Roman soldiers to prevent anyone stealing the body. There are several accounts of Jesus appearing to the disciples, and from these it seems that the Resurrection was not just the renewal of life but that the body of Jesus was changed in some way. John says that Jesus entered a room where the door was shut (John 20:19-26). Luke tells the story of two disciples who walked to Emmaus, about seven miles from Jerusalem, and on the way were joined by Jesus whom they did not recognise until he broke bread with them (Luke 24:13-35); yet Luke also stresses that Jesus was not

Stanley Spencer's painting of the resurrection in Cookham churchyard. This is a literal representation of the resurrection of the dead.

a spirit (Luke 24:36-43). According to the Book of Acts, Jesus appeared to his disciples for 40 days, then ascended to heaven (Acts 1:1-11).

Christians believe that they will all share in the Resurrection at the second coming of Jesus, and Paul calls Jesus the "first fruits of those who have fallen asleep" (I Corinthians 15:20). He says that flesh and blood cannot inherit the Kingdom of God, so people will be given new bodies. He compares this with a seed being planted in the ground which does not look anything like what actually grows:

> What is sown is perishable, what is raised is imperishable. It is sown in dishonour, it is raised in glory. It is sown in weakness, it is raised in power. It is sown a physical body, it is raised a spiritual body.
> (I Corinthians 15:42-44).

See also *Death, Easter*.

Roman Catholic Church

See *Bible (history), Bible (use), Church (history), Church (organization), Confession, Creed*.

Rosary

A rosary is a string of beads which is used in praying. It is made of five groups of ten beads, separated from each other by single beads which are easily distinguishable to the touch, so the rosary can be used without looking at it. Attached to one of these single beads is a group of three beads, another single bead, and a cross or crucifix.

Four prayers are involved: the creed, the Lord's Prayer, the Hail Mary and a short prayer of praise, the Glory be. The prayers start at the crucifix, with the creed. The Lord's Prayer is said on the single bead, a Hail Mary on each of the group of three and a Glory be on the single which comes to the circle. The single is used again for the Lord's Prayer, a Hail Mary on each of the group of ten, and a Glory be on the single. The same single is used for another Lord's Prayer; a Hail Mary is said on each of the ten and so on around to the beginning.

There are 15 holy "mysteries" (or events) which the worshipper contemplates while saying the prayers. To think about all 15 would take three rounds of the beads, but usually only five are contemplated at one time. The first five mysteries are joyful, events connected with the birth of Jesus; the second five are sorrowful and concern his suffering and death; the third five are glorious and include the Resurrection and the taking to heaven of the Blessed Virgin Mary. Together they form a summary of the life of Jesus and his mother.

It is easier to use the rosary than it sounds. Most people can do more than one thing at once, particularly when they are repeating something they do often and which does not need very much concentration. In "saying the rosary" the worshipper's hands are occupied; part of his or her mind is saying prayers which he or she knows well, while the other part can concentrate on mental prayer or meditation. For example, while praying the first joyful mystery – the message to Mary that she was to bear the child Jesus – the worshipper might start by thinking about the story, then move on to ask, "What does this mean to me? Is God asking me to do something? Can I in some way carry Jesus to people?" So the Mystery is taken from its place in history and applied to a person's life.

See also *Creed, Jesus, Mary, Meditation, Prayer*.

Sacrament

A sacrament is a visible sign of something spiritual. In the Catholic churches there are seven sacraments: baptism, confirmation, the Eucharist, confession, marriage, ordination and unction. While it is believed that Christ instituted them all, baptism and the Eucharist are especially important because they are found in the Gospels. They are sometimes called "dominical" (from the Latin word for "Lord") because they are believed to have special authority from God. It is an important Christian belief that God became a man in Jesus, and in the sacraments Christians see God continuing to work through material things, such as the water in baptism and the bread and wine in the Eucharist (see p. 25).

Among the Protestant churches only the Quakers and the Salvation Army have no belief in sacraments, but many churches only accept baptism and the Eucharist. Christians are also divided over whether a sacrament *causes* a change, or merely symbolizes one. For example, while some Christians believe that baptism results in the forgiveness of sins and in membership of the Church, others see it as simply a *sign* of forgiveness and membership which the believer has already received through repentance and faith. The frequency with which the Eucharist in particular is celebrated also varies considerably. While in some churches it is a daily act, in others it may be celebrated only once every three months, not because it is thought to be insignificant but to show its importance.

The Salvation Army has no sacraments because it does not feel that it needs any; its members may participate in a Eucharist, however, if visiting another church. Quakers believe that all life is sacred and so they try to find God not just in special ceremonies but in their everyday life. This is in fact a similar attitude to that of Christians who lay a great deal of stress on sacraments, believing that they help to make them aware of God acting throughout their lives.

See also *Church (organization)*, *Confession*, *Eucharist*, *Initiation*, *Marriage*, *Unction*.

Saint

Throughout its history the Church has paid honour to those who have died for their faith. These men and women are called "martyrs", which comes from the Greek word for "witness". The first martyr was St Stephen, whose death is recorded in the Book of Acts (chapters 6 and 7), but there have been martyrs in this century too. Dietrich Bonhoeffer was a famous religious scholar who was hanged by the Nazis in 1945 after he had opposed them and been involved in a plot to kill Hitler. This he did because he believed it was his Christian duty.

Saints belong to every century and are noted for the holiness of their lives. In the early days of the Church they were accepted as saints by the local bishop, but today the Roman Catholic Church, for example, has a long and demanding procedure of "canonization" which must be gone through before a saint is declared. Someone has to try to find faults with the writings or actions of the proposed saint to show that he or she was not perfect; this person is called the "devil's advocate".

Saints are commemorated on the anniversary of their death, because as they are believed to have died already perfect they can go straight to heaven; the day of their death is therefore the day of their birth into heaven. This sets them apart from other Christians who are not perfect when they die, and who do not go straight to heaven. The Church of England celebrates saints' days, but does not declare anyone a saint. The Protestant churches generally believe that all Christians will go straight to heaven when they die, without needing a time of further preparation, so they do not single out certain people as saints. In the New Testament the word "saint" occurs frequently in the Epistles as another word for a Christian, and some traditions have restored its broader meaning.

"Disciple" means "follower" and usually refers to one of the 12 men whom Jesus chose to be with him during his time of teaching. "Apostle" means "one who is sent" and is again used to refer to the 12; it may also be used of the men who taught about Jesus all round the known world after his ascension to heaven. These people, together with others like the Virgin Mary who are mentioned in the New Testament, are perhaps those given most honour in the Church.

Christians may address prayers to saints. This is not the same as praying to God, but rather asking the saint to pray, because the saints are in heaven and their prayers may be more powerful.

See also *Death*, *Icon*, *Jesus*, *John the Baptist*, *Joseph*, *Mary*, *Paul*, *Peter*, *Prayer*.

Salvation

Christianity is a religion of salvation. A common theme that runs throughout Christian belief is "Jesus saves". The person saved is one who receives the grace of God, a gift of divine power and favour which is freely given. The act of salvation is revealed in the Atonement (at-one-ment), the reconciliation between God and man brought about by Jesus Christ.

Traditionally, Christians believe that as all people are sinful they can only be saved, or redeemed, through Jesus Christ's sacrificial death. While Christians believe that salvation is through Christ there are a number of theories about how this atonement came about. Some believe that Christ's death was a ransom paid to the devil; others that it was the only thing that could satisfy the just desire of God to punish sin. Christ may have accepted the punishment, which was due to sinful humanity, but by the love which Christ showed to humanity, humanity should have learned to love God more.

The Protestant tradition, in general, emphasises that salvation is by faith, not through any human works. The Roman Catholic Church believes that good works along with faith can lead to salvation.

See also *Sin*.

Sin

Christians believe that sin is something which harms their relationship with God. It can take the form of an unkind or dishonest act, the passing on of malicious gossip, the harbouring of grudges or the ignoring of someone in need of help. It may also be something which weakens a believer's relationship with God, such as not spending time in prayer and Bible reading, or not going to church. In deciding whether something is a sin or not, Christians may consult the Bible, consider the rules of their church, if it has any, and listen to their conscience.

Some churches encourage the confession of sins to a priest in absolute confidence. The priest, through the authority given to him by the Church, absolves or cleanses the person from his or her sin, normally asking them to carry out some form of penance.

Traditionally the Christian Church believes that all people are born into sin. This is called "original sin". The story of Adam and Eve in the Garden of Eden (Genesis 3) and their expulsion from it is said to be a story showing how mankind lost its special relationship with God. Following this, all human beings were born inherently sinful. This sin could only be redeemed by the life, death and resurrection of Jesus which removed sin and gave people the means to restore that close and personal relationship enjoyed in the Garden of Eden. This relationship is available to all, and is received when a person is baptized into the Christian Church.

See also *Confession, Initiation, Repentance, Salvation*.

Unction

Unction is the anointing of a person with oil, usually by a bishop or priest. In Britain kings and queens are anointed at their coronation, an ancient practice going back to the first kings of Israel. One of the anthems sung at coronations is "Zadok the priest and Nathan the prophet anointed Solomon king" (I Kings 1:45), a reference to one of the sons of King David.

The purpose of unction is to give strength through the Holy Spirit, and it is one of the seven sacraments of the Catholic Church (see p. 54). In the Orthodox Church unction is a part of baptism and confirmation and it may be used at these times in Anglican and Catholic churches too.

A further occasion on which unction is administered is when people are ill. This is based on New Testament instructions:

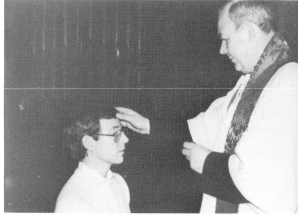

A priest anoints a man by making the sign of the cross on his forehead in colourless oil from a small container in his left hand. This anointing is taking place in church, but when people are more seriously ill it may take place at home or in hospital.

> Is any among you sick? Let him call for the elders of the church, and let them pray over him, anointing him with oil in the name of the Lord; and the prayer of faith will save the sick man, and the Lord will raise him up; and if he has committed sins, he will be forgiven.
> (James 5:14)

A person who is about to be anointed is encouraged to make a confession, as long as he is not too ill, in order to help obtain forgiveness. The oils used are blessed by a bishop. This is usually done in the cathedral on the morning of Maundy Thursday.

In churches of the Reformed traditions which do not make much use of sacraments, prayers for healing may be said while the minister lays hands on the head of the sick person. A great deal of stress may be placed on the faith of the sick person helping him or her to be healed. Jesus told the people whom he had healed that their faith was what had made them well (see Matthew 9:18-34).

See also *Holy Week, Initiation, Sacrament.*

Vestments

Vestments are special clothes which may be worn by the clergy when carrying out priestly duties during services. They are generally worn in Roman Catholic and Orthodox churches, and frequently in Anglican churches too. Elsewhere, the priest or minister may wear ordinary clothes or just a "cassock" – a long, plain, black coat with or without a white "surplice" (or black gown) and hood.

Vestments are based on the everyday clothes worn in the first centuries of the Christian Church. Between the fourth and ninth centuries men began to abandon long tunics and cloaks but they continued to be worn by priests. Nowadays, in the West, a priest celebrating the Eucharist in a church where the vestments are worn will first put on a cassock, if he is not already wearing one. Over this goes a white "alb", a long-sleeved cotton garment which reaches the ankles. A thick cotton belt or girdle, which is also usually white, is tied around the waist. Nothing so far is different from clothes which anyone may wear if they choose, and which are often worn by choristers and servers in the church. The remaining two garments are the "stole" and "chasuble", which vary in colour according to the time of year. They used to be made of heavy materials such as brocade, and were richly decorated. Many churches still use such vestments, which last a long time, but in recent years they have usually been made out of lighter materials and decorated more simply.

The stole resembles a scarf and the priest wears it around the back of his neck with the ends hanging down towards the knees. This symbolises the yoke of Christ; the stole is first worn like this when someone is made a priest. It is also worn at other times when the priest is acting in his capacity as a priest – for example at weddings, funerals, baptisms and confessions. Deacons may also wear stoles, but they wear them over their right shoulder, tied under their left arm like a sash. The chasuble resembles a poncho, with an opening for the head, and it hangs freely from the shoulders. It may be full and almost circular, if laid flat, reaching the wrists and knees, or it may be shorter and narrower, looking more like two rectangles than a circle. It is worn only by a priest celebrating the Eucharist (see pictures pp. 38-9).

This bishop is wearing very elaborate vestments. He wears a cope and mitre. The "crozier" or crook shows that he is like a shepherd to his people.

When a priest is taking a service, if he does not wear a chasuble then he may wear a "cope" – a long cloak, usually of rich material, which is fastened across the chest. It is frequently, although not exclusively, worn on happy occasions, and so is often white or yellow. Bishops usually wear a cope, together with a "mitre" – a hat which rises to a point and signifies their office. (Vestments in the Orthodox Church are different, but their origin and function are similar.)

Vestments are worn for various reasons. They have existed for centuries and so link Christians today with others through the Church's history.

They show the office of the person wearing them and emphasize that office without stressing the personality of the wearer.

See also *Year*.

Year

The Church's year begins in Advent, with a cycle which centres on Christmas, commemorating the birth of Jesus and the events connected with it – principally the visit of the wise men at Epiphany. The last event in this cycle is the Presentation of Jesus in the Temple, on 2 February, commonly called Candlemas. A second cycle centres on Easter, beginning with Ash Wednesday and ending at Pentecost. Both cycles begin with a time of preparation – Advent and Lent – when people get ready for the coming festival, although Lent is usually kept more strictly than Advent.

Outside these cycles there are many other festivals in the Christian year, celebrating either saints or events recorded in the Bible, such as the Annunciation to the Blessed Virgin Mary on 25 March. Saints are remembered on the day of their death, which is the day of their birth into heaven. The greatest honour is given to the saints of the New Testament such as John the Baptist, Peter, Paul and John. Harvest may be celebrated in the autumn and it is usual in Britain to commemorate those killed in war on the Sunday nearest to Armistice Day, 11 November, which is when the First World War ended. Individual churches usually celebrate the day of their patron saint and the anniversary of the day they were dedicated. All Saints' Day on 1 November is a general celebration of all saints, whether remembered or not, and is followed on 2 November by All Souls' Day when the dead are remembered.

The colour of items in the church made from cloth, including vestments, varies according to the season. White or "gold" is used for times of happy celebration such as Christmas, Easter and Ascension, as well as for weddings and baptisms. Red is used at Pentecost, and at times connected with blood, such as martyrs' days and Palm Sunday. Purple is used at Advent and Lent to show sorrow and repentance, as well as on Good Friday and at funerals. Some churches use rough material like sacking at Lent as a sign of Christ's uncomfortable time in the desert. Between these special times, green is used, symbolizing the

These nursery school children have lit the first candle of their Advent crown for the first Sunday in Advent. There are three more Sundays before Christmas.

continued growth of the Church. Further colours once used to be found more widely, but are now used only occasionally because there has been a move towards greater simplicity by the Church.

See also *Ascension, Christmas, Easter, Holy Week, Lent, Peter, Pentecost, Saints, Vestments*.

Midnight Mass at the Church of the Nativity in Bethlehem, celebrating Christmas at the traditional site of Christ's birth. Notice the star and the message of the angels, "*Gloria in excelsis Deo*", "Glory to God in the highest".

Important Dates in Christian History

B.C.E.	(Before the Common Era)
?4	Birth of Jesus of Nazareth.
C.E.	(Common Era)
?31	Crucifixion of Jesus.
?33	Conversion of Paul.
47-60	Paul's missionary journeys and writing of his Epistles.
60-65	Persecution of Christians in Rome by Nero.
62-64	Deaths of Peter and Paul in Rome.
70	Fall of Jerusalem and destruction of the Temple by the Romans.
70-100	Period during which Gospels, Acts of Apostles and other New Testament books were being written.
170	First mention of the four Gospels as being an accepted part of scripture.
170	Reference in Irenaeus to historical line of Bishops of Rome as the apostolic succession from Peter.
313	The Edict of Milan in which Constantine grants equal rights to Christians in the Roman Empire.
325	The Council of Nicaea – the first great Council of Bishops.
354	Birth of Augustine – one of the first leaders and theologians of the Church.
381	The Emperor Theodosius unites Church and State into one body.
432	Patrick begins missionary work in Ireland.
?550	Death of Benedict – founder of the Benedictine monastic order – whose rule forms the basis of monastic orders in the West.
563	Columba founds a monastic settlement on Iona, Scotland, after fleeing from Ireland.
597	Augustine (not the earlier one!) brings Roman Christianity to Britain.
1000	Period of building of great cathedrals starts.
1054	Final separation of eastern and western Church.
1309	The Papacy moves to Avignon (France) – threatened by the political situation in Italy.
1377	The Papacy returns to Rome.
1517	Martin Luther pins his 95 Theses to the Church door in Wittenberg and the Protestant Reformation gathers momentum.
1522	The election of the last non-Italian pope for 450 years.
1526	The first Franciscans land in Mexico.
1534	Henry VIII takes control of the Church in England.
1536	He dissolves the monasteries and disperses the religious orders.
1540	Ignatius Loyola founds the society of Jesus – the Jesuits.
1541	Jean Calvin, the French reformer, gains authority in Geneva.
1549	The first English Book of Common Prayer.
1563	The Thirty-Nine Articles define belief of the Church of England.

1570	Queen Elizabeth I is excommunicated (cut off) by the Pope.
1611	The Authorized Version of the Bible is published.
1614	The Japanese government accuses Christians of coming "to disseminate an evil law".
1620	The Pilgrim Fathers settle in Maryland, America.
1622	The Dutch set up a training institution to train missionaries to work in East Indies and Ceylon.
1643-5	The Westminster Confession – the foundation of English non-conformity.
1701	Foundation of the Anglican Society for the Propagation of the Gospel.
1703	Birth of John Wesley – the founder of Methodism.
1792	The first missionary society founded in England by the Baptists.
1795	London Missionary Society formed.
1804	British and Foreign Bible Society founded.
1815	The British allow Christians to begin missionary activity in India.
1829	The Anglican Church Missionary Society begins a major campaign to take Christianity to Africa.
1854	Pope declares the Immaculate Conception of the Virgin Mary to be an article of faith.
1858	Expansion of Christian missionary activity in Africa.
1859	The publication of Charles Darwin's *Origin of Species* fuels a debate on religion versus science.
1870	Roman Catholic Vatican Council – declaration of papal infallibility.
1889	Native Baptist Church founded in West Africa.
1907	United Methodist Church founded in Britain.
1910	First World Missionary Conference held in Edinburgh.
1932	Methodist Church of Great Britain founded.
1947	Church of South India formed bringing together Anglican, Methodist, Presbyterian and Congregational churches.
1948	World Council of Churches founded in Amsterdam.
1958	Election of Pope John XXIII.
1959	Pope summons Ecumenical Council – first since 1870.
1961	World Council of Churches' first Third World Assembly in Delhi.
1962-5	Vatican Council held – beginning of a series of reforms in the Roman Catholic Church.
1966	Pope and Archbishop of Canterbury meet in the Vatican.
1973	Lutherans and Reformed Churches agree altar fellowship under the Levenberg Agreement.
1975	World Council of Churches Assembly in Nairobi.
1981	Congregational and Presbyterian churches unite to form the United Reformed Church.
1982	Pope John Paul II visits Britain.
1986	The Pope, the Archbishop of Canterbury and leaders of other faiths met in Assisi to pray for peace.

Book List

Thinking about Christianity, R. Broadberry (Lutterworth Press, 1974)

The Christian World, A. Brown (Macdonald Educational, 1984)

Chichester Project

Christian Worship, J.C. Rankin (Lutterworth Press, 1982)

Christian Communities, A. Brown (Lutterworth Press, 1982)

Jesus, T. Shannon (Lutterworth Press, 1982)

Christian Experience, C. Erricker (Lutterworth Press, 1982)

Exploring the Bible, P. Curtis (Lutterworth Press, 1984)

The Christian's Book, P. Curtis (Lutterworth Press, 1984)

Christmas and Easter, T. Shannon (Lutterworth Press 1984)

Christian Ethics, C. Erricker (Lutterworth Press, 1984)

The Eucharist, J.C. Rankin (Lutterworth Press, 1985)

Christianity, P. Curtis (Lutterworth Press, 1986)

"Visiting a . . ." series

Visiting a Methodist Church, J. Bates (Lutterworth Press, 1984)

Visiting a Salvation Army Citadel, M. Blackwell (Lutterworth Press, 1984)

Visiting a Community Church, G. Palmer (Lutterworth Press, 1981)

Visiting a Roman Catholic Church, D. Sullivan (Lutterworth Press, 1981)

Visiting an Anglican Church, S. Tompkins (Lutterworth Press, 1981)

The Orthodox Church, S. Hackel (Ward Lock, 1971)

The Quakers, H. Hay (Ward Lock, 1981)

Roman Catholicism, P. Kelly (Ward Lock, 1971)

Protestant Christian Churches, M. Ward (Ward Lock, 1970)

Shrove Tuesday, Ash Wednesday and Mardi Gras, M. Davidson (R.M.E.P., 1984)

Holy Week, N. Fairbairn and J. Priestley (R.M.E.P., 1984)

Harvest and Thanksgiving, J. Priestley and H. Smith (R.M.E.P., 1985)

Six Religions in the Twentieth Century, W.O. Cole and P. Morgan (Hulton Educational, 1984)

The Phenomenon of Christianity, N. Smart (Collins, 1974)

Dictionary of Religions, J. R. Hinnels (Penguin, 1984)

Jesus: An Enquiry, D. Naylor and A. Smith (Macmillan Education, 1985)

The Westhill Project R.E. 5-16 series, G. Read, J. Rudge and R. Howarth (Mary Glasgow, 1986, 1987)

Festivals in World Religions, A. Brown (Shap Working Party) (C.R.E., 1987)

The Shap Handbook on World Religions in Education, ed. A. Brown (Shap Working Party) (C.R.E., 1987)

Religions, A. Brown, J. Rankin and A. Wood (Longmans, 1988)

The Christian Faith and its Symbols, J. Thompson (Edward Arnold, 1979)

Christianity in Words and Pictures, S. Thorley (R.M.E.P., 1984)

Index

Hail Mary 40, 54
harvest 58
healing 9, 56-7
heaven 23
hell 23
hermit 18
Holy Communion *see* Eucharist
Holy Spirit 9, 28-9, 46-7
Holy Week 29-31, 35, 56-7
hot cross bun 31
hymn 43-4

icon 50, 31, 16, 55
iconostasis 16
Ignatius Loyola 19
Immaculate Conception 40
incense 5, 7, 32
infant dedication 33
initiation 56, 54, 32-4, 46, 56
intercession 25, 50
Iona 19

Jesuits 19
Jesus 4, 10-12, 23-4, 25-7, 28-9, 29-31, 34-5, 36, 40, 47, 50, 53-4
Joachim 40
John the Baptist 34, 36
Joseph 11-12, 34, 36, 40, 55
Judas Iscariot 35
judgment 23

Last Supper 25-7, 29-30
Lectionary 7
Lent 20, 34, 38, 58
letters 5, 7, 46
liturgy 7, 25-7, 38-9, 50-2
Lord's Prayer 50, 54
Lord's Supper 27
Lourdes 41, 48-9
Lutheran Churches 12-13, 15
Luther, Martin 12

Magnificat 7
Mardi Gras 38
marriage 39, 54
martyr 45, 55
Mary 11-12, 34-5, 36-7, 40-1, 48-9, 54, 55
mass *see* Eucharist
Maundy Thursday 29-30, 35, 56
meditation 41, 54
meeting houses 17
memorial service 28
mercy seat 17
Messiah 35
Methodist churches 13, 14-15, 16, 25, 34, 43, 52
Metropolitan 14
minister 14-15
ministry 14
missal 50
missionary 41-2, 46

mitre 57
monk 18
monstrance 5
morality 42-3
music 43-4

Nazareth 34, 36
Nazirite 36
New Testament 5, 7, 46
Nicene Creed 21
Nunc Dimittis 7, 8
nuns 18

office 7, 19, 50, 52
oils 30, 34, 56
Old Testament 5, 7
ordination 14, 46, 54
organ 15, 43
Orthodox churches 7, 7-8, 10-12, 12-13, 14, 16, 20, 21, 22, 23-4, 25-7, 31, 32, 32-4, 38, 40, 41, 43, 50, 56, 57

Padre 14
Palm Sunday 29, 35
parable 44-5
parish 14
Passion 29, 31
pastor 15
Patriarch 14
patron 16, 45-6, 55, 58
Paul 46, 5, 55
penance 20
penitent 20
Pentecost 9, 28, 46-7, 58
Pentecostal churches 9, 13, 25, 33
Peter 5, 46, 47-8, 48
pew 15
pilgrimage 41, 48-8
pool 16
Poor Clares 19
Pope 5, 14, 47-8
prayer 35, 41, 50, 50-1, 54, 55
prayer books 25-7, 38, 50, 50-1
preaching 25-7, 52
presentation *see* Candlemas
priest 14, 20, 27
Protestant churches 5, 5-6, 7, 9, 12-13, 16-17, 21, 25, 25-7, 27-8, 39, 41, 50, 54-5, 55, 56, 56-7
province 14
psalms 7
pulpit 15-16
purgatory 23

Quakers *see* Society of Friends

reconciliation 20, 55
redemption 55-6
Reformation 12
reincarnation 28
repentance 20, 36, 53, 56, 58
Requiem Mass 28

reserved sacrament 15-16, 31
Resurrection 23, 23-4, 53-4
Roman Catholic Church 4-5, 5, 7, 7-8, 10-12, 12-13, 14-15, 15-16, 20, 21, 23-4, 25, 25-7, 17-18, 29-31, 32, 32-4, 38, 39, 40, 41, 43, 46, 47-8, 50, 50-1, 52, 54-5, 55, 55-6, 56, 57-8
Rosary 40, 41, 50, 54

sacrament 14, 20, 25-7, 32-4, 39, 54, 56
sacristy 16
saint 8, 16, 23, 31, 36, 40, 45, 46, 47, 48, 50, 55, 58
salvation 29, 55, 56
Salvation Army 13, 17, 27, 34, 43, 55
seasons *see* Year
Second Coming 35, 54
see 14
sermon 25-7
Shrove Tuesday 38
sin 20, 53, 55, 56
Society of Friends 13, 17, 27, 43, 55
Son of God 35, 28
Stations of Cross 16
statues 16
steeple 16
stole 57
suffragan 14
superintendant 15

tabernacle 16
Taizé 19
Ten Commandments 17
Tertiary 19
thurible 32
tongues, speaking in 9
tower 16
Trinity 28

unction 30, 34, 54, 56
United Reformed Church 13, 25

Veneration of Cross 31
vestments 57-8
vestry 16
vicar 14
Virgin Birth 40
votive candles 8
vows 19

Walsingham 40, 49
washing of feet 30
Week of Prayer for Christian Unity 18, 25
Wesley, Charles 43
Whitsun(day) 46
World Council of Churches 25
worship 5, 7, 25-7, 32, 38-9, 43-4, 50, 52

Year 4, 10-12, 23-4, 29-31, 38, 46-7, 55, 58-9